The Wealth Report-2

Edited by
Frank Field

Routledge & Kegan Paul

London, Boston, Melbourne and Henley

First published in 1983
by Routledge & Kegan Paul plc
39 Store Street, London WC1E 7DD,
9 Park Street, Boston, Mass. 02108, USA,
296 Beaconsfield Parade, Middle Park,
Melbourne, 3206, Australia, and
Broadway House, Newtown Road,
Henley-on-Thames, Oxon RG9 1EN
Set in 10/12pt Press Roman by
Columns Reading
and printed in Great Britain by
Thetford Press Ltd, Thetford, Norfolk

Library of Congress Cataloging in Publication Data
(Revised for volume 2)

The Wealth report.

Bibliography: v. 1, p.
Includes index.
1. Wealth — Great Britain — Addresses, essays,
lectures. 2. Income distribution — Great Britain
— Addresses, essays, lectures. I. Field,
Frank, 1942-   . II. Series.
HC260.W4W4   339.4'1'0941   78-41078

ISBN 0-7100-9452-3

The
Wealth Report-2

18/40.

£ 3-50
g

Inequality in Society

General Editor: Frank Field

Contents

Tables

Preface

I want to thank Joan Hammell for typing my contributions, the bibliography and the index. I also want to thank Rob Clements and Bob Twigger and the House of Commons Library for their help with various of the calculations which appear in the Introduction and Chapter 3, as well as Alister Sutherland for his comments on the Introduction. I alone remain responsible for the use made of the calculations and advice which was offered.

Frank Field
Birkenhead
28 January 1983

Contributors

Anthony Christopher, the General Secretary of Inland Revenue Staff Federation since 1977, is also a member of the TUC's General Council, Economic Committee and Employment Policy and Organisation Committee. He has been Chairman of NACRO (The National Association for the Care and Resettlement of Offenders) since 1973. He was a member of the Royal Commission on the Distribution of Income and Wealth 1978-9 and has been a member of the Independent Broadcasting Authority since 1978. He is joint author of 'Policy for Poverty' and contributed to 'The Wealth Report' (1979).

Frank Field has been MP for Birkenhead since 1979, and was previously from 1969 to 1979 director of the Child Poverty Action Group. In 1974 he founded the Low Pay Unit. His publications include the editing of 'Twentieth Century State Education'; 'Black Britons'; 'Low Pay'; 'Are Low Wages Inevitable?'; 'Education and the Urban Crisis'; 'The Conscript Army: a study of Britain's unemployed'; 'The Wealth Report'; and he is author of 'Unequal Britain'; 'Inequality in Britain: freedom welfare and the state'; 'Poverty and Politics'; and jointly with Chris Pond and Molly Meacher of 'To him who hath: a study of poverty and taxation'.

Clive Playford is a research officer at the Docklands Forum in London and was previously a research officer at the Low Pay Unit.

Chris Pond is Director of the Low Pay Unit. He was previously a lecturer in economics at the Civil Service College and research officer at the Low Pay Unit. His publications include: 'To Him Who Hath' (jointly); 'Trade Unions and Taxation' (jointly); 'Taxing Wealth Inequalities' (jointly); 'Taxation and Social Policy' (joint ed.); and, as editor, 'Wage Inequalities in Britain'.

Mike Reddin is a lecturer in Social Administration at the London School of Economics, with a broad range of interests in the teaching of social policy and of income maintenance in particular. His research has included work on means-testing and more recently on relations between the State and occupational pension schemes. He is author of 'Universality and Selectivity: Strategies in Social Policy' and of various chapters on pensions, taxation and occupational welfare.

Alister Sutherland is Fellow and Lecturer in Economics, Trinity College, Cambridge, and University Lecturer, University of Cambridge. Scholar of Leeds Grammar School, St John's College, Oxford and Nuffield College, Oxford. English-Speaking Union Fellow, Yale University, 1959. Lecturer at Wesleyan University, USA, and University College, London. Economic Consultant in Economic Section, HM Treasury, 1964-66. Consultancy for Board of Trade, Department of the Environment, Office of Fair Trading, etc. Economic Assessor to Greater London Development Plan Inquiry (Layfield), and to Committee on Agricultural Land (Northfield). Author of 'The Monopolies Commission in Action' (1969), and of articles on industry, competition and mergers policy, and taxation.

Dorothy Wedderburn was Professor of Industrial Sociology and Head of the Department of Social and Economic Studies at Imperial College and is now Principal of Bedford College. From 1974 to 1978 she was a member of the Royal Commission on the Distribution of Income and Wealth and her publications include, as author: 'White Collar Redundancy'; 'Redundancy and the Railwayman'; 'Enterprise Planning for Change'; 'The Economic Circumstances of Old People' (with J.E.G. Utting); 'The Aged in the Welfare State' (with Peter Townsend); 'Old Age in Three Industrial Societies' (jointly); 'Workers' Attitudes and Technology' (with Rosemary Crompton); and, as editor, 'Poverty, Inequality and Class Structure'.

Introduction:
the politics of wealth

Frank Field

This is the second volume of the 'Wealth Report' series, the
aim of which is to redress the balance of a debate which has
concentrated for far too long on looking at the poor to an almost
total exclusion of the rich. The first volume took as its theme
R.H. Tawney's view that, 'what thoughtful rich people call the
problem of poverty, thoughtful poor people call with equal
justice the problem of riches' (Tawney, 1913). This second
volume presents the latest information on that small select
group of private individuals who own a large part of Britain's
assets. More particularly, it looks at how new privileges are
being created and old ones entrenched and magnified.

This introduction begins by briefly reviewing some of the
evidence presented by the contributors to describe the extent
and persistence of wealth. It examines some of the key changes
brought about by the Thatcher government and some of the
existing, limited mechanisms of redistribution. It goes on to
examine why so little progress has been made to spread wealth
more evenly in the country and concludes by proposing three
major reforms which, together, aim at achieving a major redistributive impact.

THE OVERALL PICTURE

The first two chapters of the volume describe the pattern and
extent of wealth inequalities. In the first chapter Chris Pond
presents the latest information we have on the ownership of
wealth. The richest 1 per cent of the adult population - or the
top 400,000 or so individuals - own 4 to 5 times as much marketable wealth as the least rich 50 per cent of the population.
When the richest 2 per cent is considered the share of the rich
rises to about a third of Britain's wealth. The richest 5 per

cent between them account for half of the entire country's
wealth-holdings.

Chris Pond's and Clive Playford's joint contribution in Chapter 2 questions the conventional view that there has been a
substantial movement towards greater equality in income during
the post-war period. The official statistics do not support the
view often put over by the mass media of an inexorable grind
towards greater equality. In fact the richest 10 per cent, who
cornered a third of all incomes in 1949, maintained their share
at a little over a quarter in 1978-9. Yet the official data take
no account of the growth of non-monetary rewards (fringe
benefits for top executives, for example, are now valued at
around 30 per cent of their salary), the differential impact of
inflation (from 1956 to 1974 prices for the lowest paid rose 31
percentage points more than for higher income groups), or the
growth in tax evasion and avoidance (evasion is estimated by
the Chairman of the Inland Revenue to be in the region of $7\frac{1}{2}$
per cent of gross domestic product (GDP)). Each of these
factors has grown in importance over the past twenty years
or so and may well have offset much of the greater income
equality recorded in the official statistics.

It is against this background that we need to review changes
brought about by the Thatcher administration. Three key
changes are examined in Chapters 3 to 6 - in income tax, in
the taxation of wealth and the postponement of the rating
system's revaluation. Chapter 3 looks at the changes in taxes
on incomes, by far the most significant of which were made in
the 1979 budget. Higher rate taxpayers - 7 per cent of the
total - gained £1.6 billion in tax reductions and this concession
will continue until they are reversed by a future budget.

The Thatcher administration has abolished capital taxation
in all but name. Alister Sutherland, in Chapter 4, looks at the
rather spurious arguments used by the agricultural lobby to
justify and advance the tax advantages given to those owning
agricultural wealth. An essential part in this propaganda war
has been the argument that capital tax concessions are necessary in order to prevent the break-up of farms, and that this
is necessary because such a change would, in itself, lead to a
lowering of farm efficiency. Sutherland effectively undermines
this argument, and shows that the changes in the Capital
Transfer Tax (CTT) in the 1981 budget mean that family farms
of average size or below (valued at about a third to half a
million pounds) now pay zero CTT. Moreover, the tax concessions for transfers at death are so generous that only the
extremely rich will need to take advantage of the lifetime
transfers. But, of course, these concessions do not relate only
to agricultural wealth and elsewhere Alister Sutherland has
commented on the scope of recent capital tax reforms.

In the budget of March 1981 the Chancellor made changes
which will produce a dramatic reduction in the real burdens

of most potential payers of capital transfer tax (CTT).
Even without sophisticated tax avoidance, over 99 per cent
of wealth owners will now be able to pay zero CTT when
they hand on their assets. The burden to be borne by most
of the remaining 1 per cent has been greatly reduced.
(Sutherland, 1981, p. 37)

The 1982 budget has made further concessions to the basis of
CTT by raising the threshold by £5,000 (to £55,000) and by
easing the rate bands. As a result CTT revenue is expected to
fall from £470 million to £465 million over the next financial
year. Moreover, the capital gains tax has been further eroded
by the moderation of future gains, with no increase in the tax
rates.

The Thatcher administration has also brought about a further
redistribution of the tax burden by vetoing the 1982 rates
revaluation. Although Anthony Christopher, in Chapter 6,
looks at the threefold redistribution brought about by this
decision, the means by which the redistribution is brought
about can be seen from a summary of just one of his examples.
In respect of shops, the 'Investors Chronicle' Hillier Parker
Rent Index shows that those in prime locations have performed
something like twice as well as those elsewhere. The lack of a
revaluation here has meant that the rates burden - which
should reflect rent levels - has moved against those occupying
smaller shop premises in secondary location. Anthony Christopher observes that, to the extent that the final incidence
of rates falls on the landlords, the lack of a revaluation results
in a hidden subsidy to landlords of prime sites at the expense
of other ratepayers.

Redistribution of resources is, however, also brought about
in other, less dramatic, but by no means unimportant ways.
In Chapter 7 Mike Reddin considers what is likely to become
an increasingly important redistributing force - namely,
national insurance and occupational pension schemes. The difference the new state pension scheme will make to the living
standards of some pensioners can be seen from the following
comment by Sue Ward. 'It [the new scheme] does nothing for
people who are already retired so they will always be poorer
than the "new pensioners". In 1998, a pensioner aged 85 will
have about half the pension of many pensioners aged 65'
(Ward, 1981, p. 15).

In addition, Mike Reddin directs our attention to what will
be some of the less well-known redistributionary consequences
of the new state pension scheme. He makes some arbitrary
assumptions about levels of contributions and length of pension
life to illustrate the likely consequences. The least advantageous
group of claimants will be the single male pensioner. Married
couples will be treated more favourably and, with the greater
longevity of women over men, women on average benefit more
than their husbands, and considerably more than single male

pensioners. Given what we know about the distributional impact
of taxation which has moved in favour of single people and
against families over the past twenty to thirty years, the state
pension scheme can be seen, perhaps unintentionally, as
attempting to redress the balance somewhat.

WHY SO LITTLE CHANGE?

In an age of universal franchise why is it that wealth remains
so unequally distributed? Part of the answer is, as Chris Pond
suggests in the first chapter, that the extent and the extremities of wealth inequality defies comprehension, that without
such comprehension it is difficult to build the basis for political
change and the lack of a political challenge itself helps to
legitimise the status quo. Pond describes what can best be
thought of as a cycle of privilege whereby wealth begets
income and opportunity, status and power, and from each of
these springs wealth.
  But this still does not explain why the issue is low in priori-
ties of Left politicians. Much of the current debate in the
Labour Party is dominated by discussions on the Alternative
Economic Strategy and withdrawal from Europe. Demand for
fiscal changes - even in respect of wealth - has a faint whiff
of the political past about it. This is in part, no doubt, a
reaction against Gaitskellite revisionism which was seen by its
opponents as little more than tinkering around with the tax
system, and which, when tried under a Wilson government,
failed to bring forth any major structural changes.
  A policy of guilt by association has led to a downgrading in
the political importance of fiscal changes and this has resulted
in all too little effort being given to thinking through such
issues while in opposition. In the first volume of 'The Wealth
Report', Cedric Sandford writes that, during the 1970-4
parliament, Labour undertook very little serious study of its
proposal to introduce a wealth tax (for example, was it to
replace investment income surcharge or to redistribute existing wealth?) and even less on the mechanics of its operation
(Sandford, 1979).
  The failure to realise the importance of redistributing wealth
allowed the 1974 Labour government to side-track itself into
establishing a fact-gathering Royal Commission on the Distribution of Income and Wealth which issued not a single recom-
mendation during its entire life - although, as Dorothy Wedderburn's contribution shows, it provides a mass of new statistical
data and represented existing information in a regular and
powerful way. Indeed, Lord Diamond, the Chairman of the
Royal Commission, favoured this more limited role and defended
the Commission's fact-gathering exercise in the following
terms:

You have the great advantage that when you have a body
of people with diverse views, diverse philosophies, diverse
backgrounds, diverse attitudes, coming to a single conclusion about a set of figures, the authority and objectivity
which that imparts to their findings is enormous, so long
as they don't try to draw conclusions from it .... The very
fact that you are not required to make and do not make
recommendations adds to the credibility of the facts which
you produce. (Bulmer, 1980, p. 163)

Even if this was thought to be the best political use of a
Royal Commission, the Labour government failed to utilise
what Lord Diamond termed 'the authority and objectivity' of
the Commission's findings. At no time did any member of the
government seek to introduce the electorate to the Commission's
main findings. Nor, on a more modest scale, were the reports
used to counter-attack the Tory charges of Labour's rampant
egalitarianism which dominated the long run-up to the 1979
election. Many of the wilder charges made by the Opposition
could have been countered by the information in the Royal
Commission reports, but I can recall no occasion when a single
Labour minister used a single shred of evidence from any one
of the Commission's reports.

WHAT IS TO BE DONE?

Reflecting on her experience on the Royal Commission,
Dorothy Wedderburn's advice to the next Labour government
is to begin redistributing wealth and not to make the redistribution of income the first major political initiative of the government. But how is one to build up enough support to raise the
question of redistributing wealth in the political pecking order?
  In part this may come by the careful dissemination of information as to who owns what in Britain today - which is the
purpose of these wealth reports. It is also important to link
this campaign with an explanation of how the great concentrations of wealth are acquired in our society. Both Chris Pond
and, to some extent, Alister Sutherland emphasise that the
holdings of the very rich have far more to do with inheritance
than enterprise, initiative or hard work. The evidence presented
in Pond's chapter on this point reinforces earlier work by
Tony Atkinson. In the early 1970s Atkinson showed that it
would take a worker, on average earnings, 2,000 years to
amass capital of £2½ million (Atkinson, 1972, p. 45), and a
decade later little has changed. Updating Atkinson's £2½ million
figure in today's money gives a sum of £13 million which it
would take a person on average earnings just over 2,000 years
to earn.
  More importantly, the Royal Commission presented information
on what would be the likely distribution of wealth if acquisition

was based on savings over a person's lifetime - key data for
any educational campaign in the country on the importance of
redistributing the nation's wealth. The information is presented
in Table I.1 below and shows that, on the basis of accumulated
savings, the richest 1 per cent could be expected to possess
on various calculations between 3 per cent and 6.9 per cent of
the nation's wealth, whereas they owned in reality 22.5 per
cent. If ownership of wealth was governed by past savings,
the bottom 80 per cent (and it is only in matters of wealth
distribution does one ever see reference to the bottom 80 per
cent of a distribution) could have been expected to possess a
little over 40 per cent of the nation's wealth, whereas four-
fifths of the population owned less than 24 per cent of the
nation's assets.

TABLE I.1   *Distribution of accumulated savings out of earnings from*
employment and the distribution of total wealth

| | Distribution of Accumulated Savings | | | Actual Distribution of Wealth |
| | (1) | (2) | (3) | (4) |
	Atkinson	Flemming	RCDIW	Inland Revenue
Top 1 per cent	3.0	5.5	6.9	22.5
Top 2.5 per cent	11.2	11.0	16.6	20.6
Top 6.10 per cent	12.9	na	14.7	14.4
Top 11.20 per cent	na	na	21.3	18.8
Bottom 80 per cent	na	na	40.5	23.7

Notes: (1) Atkinson — assumes realistic lifetime earnings with 4½ per cent interest.
(2) Flemming — allows for different earnings streams. (3) RCDIW — by age, sex and two
social class groups, assumes compound interest of 4 per cent. (4) Inland Revenue (C) Series
1974. na — not available.
(*Source*: Royal Commission Report No. 5, 1977, and Royal Commission Report No. 7,
1979.)

What sort of tax reforms need to follow on from a campaign
which explains how most wealth is acquired in Britain today?
Three reforms are important. The first should concentrate on
closing the loopholes, if that is not too mild an expression, in
the Capital Transfer Tax provisions. At the very least this
will mean the rescinding of all the major structural changes
which have been made to the tax since its inception. There
is also the need to begin questioning the range of the concessions given to agricultural and business wealth-holders in
framing the original measure. Most of these reforms to the CTT
are ones which could be enacted in the first Finance Act of a
new parliament controlled by a new anti-Tory majority. If an

extended period of negotiations is necessary on some of the
changes to the taxation of agricultural wealth, the first Finance
Act should begin the process of reform and give a clear indica-
tion on reviewing the effectiveness of the CTT each year.
  A second reform should centre on turning CTT into an accessions tax (Sandford et al., 1973). While CTT is based on the
idea of taxing wealth as it is transferred, the tax base is
linked to the assets of the person giving the wealth, rather
than the assets of those who are the beneficiaries. If one of
the aims of the tax is to spread wealth more evenly, then it is
clearly desirable to build into its arrangements a sliding scale
whereby the tax becomes proportionately greater the larger
is the wealth of the donee and vice versa.
  It is also crucial to get clear how comprehensive the accessions tax should be. It is important that it will cover all gifts
and legacies. Similarly, to be most effective, the tax needs
to be based on a lifetime accumulation rather than CTT's
current ten-year period. It is also important that the new
accessions tax goes to the root of wealth inequality. In this
volume and elsewhere we find evidence of how heavily concentrated wealth is within certain families, and that what
redistribution there has been recently has occurred between
members of rich families, rather than between rich and poorer
families. This being so, Richard Wainwright is surely right
to argue for not incorporating any consanguinity relief in an
accessions tax (Wainwright, 1981). Moreover, as some of the
largest wealth-holdings are held in trusts, a periodic capital
levy must be applied to such wealth-holdings.
  The third reform should centre on the introduction of a
wealth tax. But what form should this wealth tax take? Cedric
Sandford makes a distinction between those tax proposals
which are 'confiscatory' and which must necessarily be paid
largely from capital and other proposals which, because they
are aimed at substituting a wealth tax for the investment
income surcharge, can be paid from existing income (Sandford,
1971). In the former category comes the 1977 Labour Party/
TUC Liaison Committee proposal for a graded tax, starting at
1 per cent on wealth valued between £100-300,000 rising to
5 per cent on wealth of five million pounds or more. This rate
structure effectively omits 99 per cent of the adult population
from those liable to the tax.
  A much more redistributive proposal was advanced by the
TUC almost a decade earlier when it advocated a tax on property
over £10,000 at an average rate of 3 per cent. If this proposal
is up-dated to account for inflation then, at the latest for
which wealth statistics are available (1977), we find that the
starting point of the tax rises to £50,000 and that over 96 per
cent of the population is exempt. On optimistic assumptions this
reform would have brought in an additional £1,000 million
revenue.
  Sandford, writing in the early 1970s, was concerned to show

that this proposal, when combined with the income tax rates
and allowances in 1967-8, became confiscatory even on quite
low wealth-holdings. He illustrated this by way of assuming a
5 per cent gross return on capital and a flat rate 3 per cent
wealth tax. The combined effect of income and wealth taxation
on these assumptions was a marginal rate of over 100 per cent
on wealth-holdings in excess of £25,000. At approximately
£70,000 the combined amount of income and wealth taxes
exceeded 100 per cent of income, i.e. the tax structure is
confiscatory. Up-dating this example to 1981-2 shows marginal
rates of 100 per cent and over being effective on wealth holdings above £140,000 and average rates of 100 per cent on
wealth over about £350,000. Allowing for inflation (retail prices
in 1981-2 were about five times their 1967-8 level) shows that
the current tax system is only slightly less progressive than
that in 1967-8. However, it is at the highest rates of tax that
the effects of the Thatcher administration's 1979 tax changes
can be seen. After four years of a Thatcher government
favouring the very rich at the expense of practically the whole
community, is it too much to ask a future radical government to
have the will to redistribute at a confiscatory rate on wealth
holdings valued at more than a £$^{1}/_{3}$ million in 1981-2?

CONCLUSION

The weight of evidence and experience shows how difficult it
will be to win support for these three critical reforms -
particularly the last. There is, first, the problem of explanation. What little information we have suggests that a wealth
tax is not seen by the electorate to be either a compelling
vote-catcher or an obvious political priority (Sandford et al.,
1978). The urgent need is, therefore, to open a wider political
debate on the issue. This volume of 'The Wealth Report' series,
with its emphasis on the impact of policy will, I hope, not only
prompt this debate, but will prepare the ground for more
informed democratic argument, and, ultimately, for action.

Wealth and the two nations*

Chris Pond

Britain is a deeply divided society, and the deepest division of all is the inequality in the ownership of wealth. That the inequalities have persisted for so long helps in itself to legitimate them, to make them more acceptable; the status quo is an influential public relations officer for the rich. And the very extremities of wealth inequalities somehow deprive the statistics of credibility or meaning. They defy comprehension, let alone challenge. Yet the truth is that inequality feeds upon itself. Wealth begets income and opportunity, status and power; and from each of these springs wealth. The inequalities are circular and self-perpetuating.

In the first part of this chapter we examine the changes that have taken place in the distribution of personal wealth between the first quarter and last of this century. We then examine the nature of wealth inequalities as they manifest themselves today, and explore the explanations that have been offered for their persistence. The second part of the chapter turns towards the system of wealth taxation in Britain. Why have capital taxes, described by Sir Geoffrey Howe, the Conservative Chancellor as 'capricious and sometimes savage levies', had such a limited impact on wealth inequalities? And what reforms would be required to secure a more effective role for such taxation in future? We begin by looking back to the 1920s, the years of Gatsby and Bloomsbury. How much more equal is Britain today?

THE GALLOP TOWARDS EQUALITY?

Measurement of the size and nature of a problem, without the intention even when the information is available to do very much about it, is an exercise which lacks a sense of purpose. It is perhaps unsurprising, therefore, that official statistics are still unable to describe conclusively the true extent of wealth inequalities. The statistics, like those on the distribution of income, are a by-product of the administrative process of tax collection. Wealth in Britain, for most of this century, has only been taxed when its owner dies, so that estimates of total wealth holdings are based on a relatively small sample each year. And since wealth-holders have to be either very rich, or very careless, or both, for their wealth to pass through the estate duty office at all, estimates of the true magnitude of wealth inequalities require some elaborate, and not always wholly reliable, adjustments. Partly for this reason, as Dorothy Wedderburn recalls in Chapter 4, the Royal Commission on the Distribution of Income and Wealth, established as part of the last Labour government's commitment 'to shift the balance of wealth and power in favour of working people and their families', spent most of its time working out what the current balance of wealth and power actually was. The Commission was left with little time to consider what should be done about the situation, even if it had wished to do so.

For the most part it has been left to independent academics and researchers to estimate the distribution of wealth, and how it has changed. Prominent amongst these are A.B. Atkinson and A.J. Harrison. It is their work which has provided us, very recently, with the most consistent statistics on wealth inequalities stretching back over half a century, from the early 1920s to the early 1970s. Although, as the authors make clear, the series is still subject to certain discontinuities, and the actual magnitude of the figures should be treated with caution, these are the most reliable statistics yet made available. They suggest that, although the share of the top 1 per cent of wealth-holders has declined, the rate of decline has been very much less than previous estimates, including those used by the Royal Commission, would lead us to believe. The estimates are given in the table below.

The Royal Commission's figures had suggested that the share of the richest 1 per cent of wealth-holders had fallen over this period at a rate of 0.7 per cent a year – hardly a gallop. But the more consistent series compiled by Atkinson and Harrison show that the rate of decline was little more than half that suggested by the orthodox presentation. Over the entire period 1923 to 1972, the share of the richest 1 per cent declined at an annual rate of only 0.4 per cent, subject to a once-for-all jump in 1959 and 1960. Contrary to the established view, there has been no apparent acceleration in the arithmetic rate of decline. It follows that, by the end of this century, if change continues at this rate, the top 1 per cent can still look forward to owning almost a fifth of all the personal wealth. Even in the year 2020 they will still enjoy a tenth of the nation's wealth.

The more wealthy of our readers may still be alarmed at this prospect, and we should point out that, on the basis of the more recent figures, the share of the richest groups is

TABLE 1.1 *Distribution of wealth in England and Wales 1923-72*

	Top 1%	Top 5%	Top 10%	Top 20%	Bottom 80%
1923	60.9	82.0	89.1	94.2	5.8
1928	57.0	79.6	87.2	93.1	6.9
1938	55.0	76.9	85.0	91.2	8.8
1950	47.2	74.3	–	–	–
1953	43.6	71.1	–	–	–
1958	41.4	67.8	–	–	–
1960	33.9	59.4	71.5	83.1	16.9
1965	33.0	58.1	71.7	85.5	14.5
1968	33.6	58.3	71.6	85.1	14.9
1970	29.7	53.6	68.7	84.5	15.5
1971	28.4	52.3	67.6	84.2	15.8
1972	31.7	56.0	70.4	84.9	15.1

Source: Table 6.5, Atkinson and Harrison (1978).

unlikely to continue falling at even this pedestrian pace. The estimates suggest that, by the mid-1960s, the rate of decline had evaporated altogether. The authors calculate that the downward trend in their estimates between 1966 and 1972 was not significantly different from zero when statistical tests of significance are applied. As one of the authors reported in the first edition of 'The Wealth Report':

> the errors introduced as a consequence of estimating the distribution of wealth from a sample could alone explain all the variations observed in the share of the top one per cent over the period. Overall, the safest conclusion is that the distribution of wealth in the early 1970s was little different from that observed in the early 1960s. (Harrison, 1979, p. 40)

The rate of decline in the share of wealth monopolised by the very richest individuals appears to have been much slower than had previously been assumed. Moreover, while the share of the top 1 per cent has been slowly declining, that of the richest four per cent immediately below them has remained constant. In other words, the decline has been confined to the share of the richest one per cent. As Atkinson explained in an earlier work 'what redistribution there has been is not between the rich and the poor, but between the very rich and the rich' (Atkinson, 1972, p. 22). We will return to an explanation of this phenomenon in a moment.

Overall, therefore, the share of wealth enjoyed by the richest 1 per cent has almost halved over the period of half a century considered. But the rest of the top 5 per cent apparently increased their share marginally from just over 21 per cent to just over 24 per cent. This change is unlikely to be statistically significant but the direction of change is clear. Taking the lower half of the richest 10 per cent (the top 6-10 per cent), their share apparently doubled, from 7 per cent to over 14 per cent; and the share of the next richest 10 per cent (the top 11-20 per cent) almost trebled their proportionate wealth-holding from 5 per cent to 14½ per cent. In 1923 the top fifth of the adult population enjoyed 94 per cent of the personal wealth; in 1972 they still retained 85 per cent of the total. Such a decline may hardly be described as cataclysmic.

One explanation for this pattern of change in the relative shares of the top groups might be that the redistribution had taken place, not from the richest families, but within them. In other words, heads of household (likely to fall into the richest 1 per cent) were passing their wealth on to other members of the family (who were also numbered within the top 5 per cent) (see Atkinson, 1972, p. 23). This explanation received considerable support from an examination of a sample of estates receiving probate in 1973, carried out by the Royal Commission. Not surprisingly, the great majority of bequests were made to relatives of the deceased. The Commission concluded that: 'The fragmentation of large wealth holdings at death reduces the share of the top one per cent, but to the benefit of the groups immediately below as a number of beneficiaries each receives a sizeable bequest' (Royal Commission Report No. 5, 1977, para. 399). This, of course, is redistribution of a rather special kind, representing little more than the re-ordering of affairs within the richest families, possibly to minimise the impact of death duties. The poor gained nothing; for them, changes in the distribution of wealth between the 1920s and 1970s was little more than a spectator sport, with no prizes for the crowd.

WEALTH SHARES IN THE 1970s

The Atkinson/Harrison series presents us with a picture of changes in the distribution of wealth up until the early 1970s. Since then official estimates have become available on a much improved basis. The share of half the population was so small that the Inland Revenue previously found it difficult to measure it at all, and presented estimates on the assumption that they owned no wealth. The exclusion of half the population left the statistics open to criticism (especially from such as the Institute of Economic Affairs) that the figures dramatically overstated inequality. The adjustment of the figures yielded estimates remarkably similar to the old series. The wealth of half the population was indeed negligible.

Part (i) of Table 1.2 shows the distribution of personal wealth amongst the adult members of the UK population in the 1970s. The distribution changed very little after 1974. In each year, the richest 1 per cent of the adult population enjoyed almost one-quarter of the nation's personal wealth. We should put this in perspective. One per cent of the adult population represents slightly more than 400,000 people – the turnout normally expected at Epsom on Derby Day! This tiny handful of people owned four or five times as much wealth as the least privileged half of the population had to share between them. Two per cent of adults owned almost one-third of the wealth; 5 per cent owned almost half; and 10 per cent owned almost two-thirds.

TABLE 1.2 *Distribution of wealth 1971-9*

United Kingdom					Percentages		
	1971	1974	1975	1976	1977	1978	1979
(i) Marketable wealth							
Percentage of wealth owned by:							
Most wealthy 1 per cent of population[a]	31	23	24	24	23	23	24
Most wealthy 2 per cent of population	39	30	31	32	30	30	32
Most wealthy 5 per cent of population	52	43	44	46	44	44	45
Most wealthy 10 per cent of population	65	57	58	61	58	58	59
Most wealthy 25 per cent of population	86	84	83	84	82	83	82
Most wealthy 50 per cent of population	97	93	93	95	95	95	95
Total marketable wealth (£ thousand million)[b]	164	236	272	296	345	401	488
(ii) Marketable wealth plus occupational pension rights							
Percentage of wealth owned by:							
Most wealthy 1 per cent of population	27	19	20	21	19	19	20
Most wealthy 2 per cent of population	34	26	26	27	25	26	26
Most wealthy 5 per cent of population	46	38	38	40	38	39	38
Most wealthy 10 per cent of population	59	52	52	53	51	52	51
Most wealthy 25 (3) per cent of population	78-83	76-82	75-81	75-81	74-78	75-79	75-79
Most wealthy 50 (3) per cent of population	90-96	88-92	88-92	89-93	88-92	89-93	89-93
(iii) Marketable wealth plus occupational and state pension rights							
Percentage of wealth owned by:							
Most wealthy 1 per cent of population	21	15	13	14	12	13	13
Most wealthy 2 per cent of population	27	21	18	18	17	17	18
Most wealthy 5 per cent of population	37	31	27	27	25	25	27
Most wealthy 10 per cent of population	49	43	37	37	35	36	37
Most wealthy 25 (3) per cent of population	69-72	64-67	58-61	58-61	55-58	57-60	58-61
Most wealthy 50 (3) per cent of population	85-89	85-89	81-85	80-85	78-82	79-83	79-83

Notes: a. Aged 18 and over. b. End year. 3. Estimates vary with assumptions.
Source: 'Social Trends' 12 (1982), London, HMSO.

Such figures are still difficult to comprehend. Indeed, as we suggested above, this may be one reason why the persistence of wealth inequalities is not subjected to more rigorous public

inquiry. The figures are so extreme that, for most of the
population they have little meaning. There is an old saying:
'What you've never had, you never miss.' And since half the
population has never had more than a negligible amount of
wealth, the concept defies comprehension, let alone challenge.
The scale of the inequality becomes clearer if we consider
the actual amounts of wealth involved. In 1979, total marketable wealth was estimated at just under £500 billion. If equally
distributed, each member of the population aged over eighteen
would have had average net wealth (after paying off their
mortgages, debts and other liabilities) of around £12,000 at
1979 prices. Each household would have net wealth, on average,
of over £30,000 in 1979. The actual situation was rather different. Those in the bottom half of the distribution had average
wealth of only £1,200 each or £3,000 per household – less than a
tenth as much as if wealth had been equally shared. Meanwhile,
those in the top half of the distribution had an average wealth-
holding of £23,000 each (almost £60,000 per household). A
sharper illustration of Disraeli's 'two nations' would be difficult
to contemplate. Half the population had an average twenty times
as much wealth as the other half.
These are, of course, only averages based on the assumption
of 2.6 adults per household; we are not suggesting that all
households conform to the average composition. Nor do we
assume that the assets which make up the wealth could be easily
divided in this way. Furthermore, even amongst the richest
half of the population wealth is extremely unequally divided.
As Tony Atkinson has explained, 'the gap between Mr X who
just qualifies for the top one per cent and the millionaire with
a household name is much larger than that between Mr X and
the average wealth-holder' (Atkinson, 1975, p. 131). The
richest 1 per cent of adults owned an average of almost a
third of a million pounds or nearly £800,000 per household –
250 times as much as the average wealth-holding amongst the
least privileged half of the populace.

EXPLAINING WEALTH INEQUALITIES

The magnitude and persistence of these inequalities requires
some explanation. Recent years have seen substantial growth
of various forms of 'popular' wealth: housing, pensions,
insurance policies, national savings. Certainly, these have had
some impact. But their effect has, to a large extent, been
offset by influences operating in the opposite direction. We
should begin by examining the effect of the growth of pensions.
The analysis we have presented so far have been concerned
primarily with 'marketable' wealth – that which could be sold
and realised as cash without very much difficulty. Now it may
be argued that this definition of wealth is too narrow. We
should be concerned with an individual's 'command over

economic resources', and this goes beyond the value of his
goods and chattels. A young man, assured of a good job or
future inheritance, may well be able to persuade his bank
manager to advance him a loan now in anticipation of the day
when his ship comes in. His command over economic resources
is well in excess of his current wealth. Using similar reasoning,
the Royal Commission on the Distribution of Income and Wealth
argued that the present (capitalised) value of the future
incomes assured by an occupational or state pension should be
included in calculations of the value of wealth. Table 1.2 (ii)
shows estimates of the distribution including occupational
provisions, while Table 1.2 (iii) includes state pensions
rights. Because the estimates of the effect of this on the
wealth of the least privileged vary according to the assumptions
used about their allocation, a range of estimates are given.

The inclusion of such assets in the estimates makes a significant difference, to the actual shares, if not to trends in the
distribution during the 1970s. Including occupational pensions
reduces the overall share of the top 1 per cent from 24 to 20
per cent, and if state pension rights are also included, this
falls again to 13 per cent. The 'poorest' half of the population
are seen to gain a bigger share of wealth defined in this way.

We have to ask whether this adjustment to the figures
improves our understanding or simply helps to numb us to the
harsh facts about the distribution of marketable wealth. It is
quite correct to say that a more comprehensive definition of
wealth is desirable; but if only a small part of the additional
elements of wealth can be calculated, their inclusion may serve
only to distort the picture. For if we are to include future
rights to pensions why not also prospective inheritances,
rights to education, and to future earnings? Since rights and
opportunities normally go hand in hand with wealth and privilege, it is not at all clear that estimates based on a truly
comprehensive definition of wealth, even if they could be
calculated, would yield a distribution more equal than that of
normally defined marketable wealth.

Moreover, as Louie Burghes pointed out in the first edition
of 'The Wealth Report', there is an important difference
between occupational and state pension rights. Entitlement to
a state pension promises a flow of income at some date in the
future. The size of this flow will depend on the individual's
contribution during his/her life-time and the length of time
they live to enjoy it. Since many manual workers live only
a short time into retirement, they may be excused for scepti-
cism about their inclusion amongst the wealthy. But even those
who have entitlement to a full state pension will be unable
either to cash in this entitlement or to use it as security on a
loan. Those with occupational pension rights may enjoy both
these options. Even so, only about one third of the population
have any form of occupational pensions (Burghes, 1979,
pp. 27-8). There is no doubt, however, that other forms of

'popular' wealth should be included - housing, insurance
policies, national savings - as indeed they are in Table 2.1 (i).
These are unequivocally elements of the total stock of wealth.
And, of these, housing is, of course, the most important.

The growth in home ownership this century has been quite
dramatic. At the turn of the century only 10 per cent of
dwellings were owner-occupied. By the early 1960s this had
increased to over 40 per cent, rising again to 54 per cent by
the late 1970s. The growth in owner-occupation in itself need
not have had a major impact on the inequalities we recorded
above. We are dealing in net wealth, after taking account of
debts and liabilities, including mortgages. So the average
family can only count in its 'wealth' the amount of its home
that it actually owns - what it has 'paid off'. However, this
growth in owner-occupation has been accompanied by a very
considerable growth in house prices. Between 1960 and 1976
the price of housing rose six-fold, with a large part of this
rise occurring between 1970 and 1973. No other form of wealth
increased in value so dramatically. (Royal Commission Report
No. 8, 1979, p. 125).

As house prices increased, 'homeowners' found the value of
their wealth (net of liabilities) increasing and with it their
share of total wealth. The very poorest, who are less likely
to be amongst the owner-occupying classes, probably gained
little but the increase in owner-occupation was undoubtedly
an important social change. What is perhaps more remarkable
is the fact that this change together with the growth in other
forms of popular wealth had such a limited impact on the
overall distribution. To understand why, we need to look more
carefully at the nature of wealth inequalities.

Our discussions earlier in this chapter have been in terms of
aggregate wealth, boiling all assets down to their money value.
The top 1 per cent of the population, as we noted above,
overall owned about one-quarter of the personal wealth. But
they also owned almost 70 per cent of the personal wealth held
in the form of land, and almost half that in the form of buildings (other than dwellings). The same 1 per cent of the
population owned 70 per cent of the listed ordinary shares and
77 per cent of the other company securities, and two-thirds of
all UK government securities.

The concentration is still more remarkable when one considers
the wealth-holdings of the richest 0.1 per cent of the population. There were little more than 40,000 people in this group.
But between them they owned over 40 per cent of the private
land, a quarter of the listed ordinary shares and a third of
other company securities in private hands plus a third of UK
government securities.

Now we are in a position to examine why the growth in owner-
occupation (and other forms of 'popular wealth') have not had
more impact, why the 1950s Conservative dream of 'every man
a capitalist' has not been realised. The elements of 'popular

wealth' which are most important to those with relatively small
wealth holdings are of little significance to the very richest.

For example, those who had net wealth of less than £5000
in 1976 held virtually all of it in the form of dwellings, household goods, life policies, building society deposits, cash and
bank deposits, and national savings. By contrast, those with
net wealth exceeding £200,000 held less than a third of its
gross value in these forms. It follows from this that an increase
in house prices, for instance, will have a considerable impact
on the wealth of the least wealthy, but little on that of the
very richest. Rapid changes in the price of land or shares will
have the opposite effect. The first will tend to equalise the
distribution of wealth; the second to increase the degree of
inequality.

An illustration of how this can effect the degree of measured
inequality was provided by the Royal Commission who calculated the impact of the changing importance of different types
of assets as well as their changes in price. Over the period
1960 to 1972 for instance, the growth of owner-occupation and
mortgages as well as increasing home prices resulted in a
decline in the relative share of the top 1 per cent by 6 percentage points. But the increase in the quantity and price of stocks
and shares increased their share by $7\frac{1}{2}$ percentage points.
The two effects cancelled each other out. The net decline in
the wealth-holdings of the richest groups was attributed to an
increase in the importance of cash assets, insurance
policies and household goods.

Look again at Table 1.2 (i). At first glance the table is
puzzling. Between 1971 and 1974, a period of Conservative
rule, the share of the richest 1 per cent fell significantly,
from 31 per cent to 23 per cent of the total. After 1974, with
the election of a Labour government committed to 'a redistribution of wealth and power in favour of working people and
their families', we would have expected a further fall. Instead,
the richest wealth-holders recovered somewhat from the un-
nerving decline in their share under the previous administration. The explanation is to be found in the asset composition
of wealth and relative price changes. The early 1970s saw a
virtual collapse of the stock market, with the result that the
book value of shares was reduced 'at a stroke' (to borrow a
phrase rather popular at that time). The redistribution which
we witnessed in the 1970s was therefore of a rather special
kind. Once again the poor gained nothing from the declining
fortunes of the rich, except perhaps a little smug satisfaction.

Readers may be surprised that, in considering changes in
the distribution of wealth, we have as yet made no mention of
wealth taxation. When we come to examine the operation of
wealth taxes in detail in the next section, the reasons for this
apparent neglect will become clear: wealth taxes have been
largely irrelevant, certainly in the most recent past. In the
previous volume of 'The Wealth Report' Alan Harrison summarised

the results of his work with Tony Atkinson attempting to
assess the causes of the change in the distribution of wealth
between 1923 and 1972. Two possible conclusions emerged from
this analysis: one was that the decline in the share of the top
1 per cent was due to an increase in the importance of 'popular
wealth', offset by an increase in share prices working in the
opposite direction; the other, perhaps less plausible, explanation was that estate duty taxation had been most important
in reducing wealth inequalities, offset again by the increase in
share prices. Harrison's own assessment was that 'Estate Duty,
if it has had any influence, has conducted a "holding operation", preventing an increase in concentration' (Harrison,
1979, p. 42).

WEALTH AND POWER

An analysis of the types of asset that make up the wealth of
different groups, as shown in the previous two tables, help
us to explain why there has not been a more dramatic equalisation of wealth during the post-war period. Certainly, there
has been an increase in the importance, and value, of 'popular
wealth' - houses, insurance policies and pensions. But these
have always been of relatively little importance in the port-
folios of the very rich, and the equalisation that has taken
place has to a large extent been offset by movements in the
opposite direction.
    This type of analysis also helps us to understand the true
nature of wealth, and its importance as a social and political,
as well as economic, concept. In the earlier edition of 'The
Wealth Report', Louie Burghes drew attention to an important
distinction between different types of wealth which Professor
Halsey had identified as the distinguishing division of society:

> property for power by which I mean property which carries
> control over the lives of other people, and property for use
> - possessions that free a man from other people's con-
> trol.... A tiny minority has monopolised wealth, and an
> even tinier minority has monopolised property for power.
> (Halsey, 1978, p. 80)

What Halsey meant by this distinction becomes clear from
our discussion on the types of assets which make up wealth.
Those forms of wealth that yield an improvement in living
standards and security - houses, consumer durables, pensions,
insurance policies - all have grown. But the wealth that confers
social and political power - land, shares and company securities -
remain heavily concentrated in the hands of the few. All these
provide their owners with an ability to control not only their
own lives, but the lives of others as well. If one is to take
issue with Professor Halsey's distinction, it may be in his

assertion that the ownership of 'property for use' frees its
owner from other people's control. Such property may provide
improved living standards or security; but in itself it is unlikely to free him or her from the need to work for their living,
remaining under the control of others.

An alternative distinction between different types of wealth
has been offered by Chris Hird who argues that capital
(similar to Halsey's 'wealth for power') is the most important
element in social inequality:

> Capital ... is different from other forms of wealth: shares
> in an industrial company, for example, will typically grow
> in value over time, produce a regular dividend, confer
> legal ownership over part of the company's material assets,
> and are moreover, easily marketable when necessary. Other
> forms of wealth are quite different: consumer goods
> generally depreciate and have low second-hand value;
> the value of houses may in the main appreciate, but they
> are often difficult to sell and the owner generally needs
> to buy another as replacement; pensions provide an
> entitlement to a future income only as long as the pensioner
> lives, are not transferable, and often depreciate in value;
> and cash, although it confers immediate economic power
> through its purchasing power, generally depreciates. It
> is changes in the ownership and control of the means of
> production that need to be treated as the central criterion
> in assessing the distribution of wealth, for changes in
> other forms of wealth are intimately related to these.
> (Hird, 1979, p. 202)

Hird goes on to argue that the Royal Commission's preoc-
cupation with the distribution of personal wealth, and its
failure to distinguish between different types of personal
wealth, had caused it to overlook the major concentrations
of power in society. It is often argued, for instance, that the
growth of institutionalised wealth - in companies, pension
funds, insurance institutions and the banks - has led us
nearer to the 'property-owning democracy' by breaking the
hold on the nation's wealth of a few powerful individuals. On
the contrary, the evidence suggests that control of institutionalised wealth is still more heavily concentrated than
personal wealth. Hird cites Department of Trade evidence
to show that, even by the late 1960s, just thirty insurance
companies controlled 85 per cent of all insurance company
assets, while the biggest five companies controlled 38 per cent
(Hird, 1979, p. 203). And in these companies perhaps a handful of people have real control.

The wealth owned by the pension funds is also heavily
concentrated. It has been calculated that 40 institutions control
three-quarters of all pension fund money and that, within
these funds, perhaps just 200 people have investment authority

and control. The banks, too, represent enormous concentrations
of wealth: the 'big four' banks between them account for 70 per
cent of bank deposits (Cripps et al., 1981).

In all these cases ownership and control of this wealth has
been sieved and separated; and in the process the power
attaching to the wealth, that is (nominally) owned by many
millions of ordinary people, is transferred to those who have
control of it in its concentrated and institutionalised form. The
pension contributions and entitlements of workers, the building
society deposits and mortgages, the bank deposits and insurance
policies, none of these confer on those who 'own' them any
measure of control or power. This lies in the hands of what
have been described as 'small oligarchies of power' - the chief
executives, boards of directors, and investment managers who
determine how such wealth shall be used. While the Royal
Commission busied itself allocating the nominal ownership of
this wealth in terms of owner-occupation, pension entitlements,
insurance policies and bank deposits, it overlooked the control
of the building societies, the pension funds, the insurance
companies and the banks.

In no area is the importance of control, irrespective of ownership, more effectively illustrated than in the area of corporate
wealth. In 1979 it is estimated that the six largest industrial
concerns listed on the London Stock Exchange accounted for
over one-quarter of the turnover, while the top 180 accounted
for 80 per cent. Just over 150 industrial concerns accounted
for 30 per cent of the output and for the same proportion of net
tangible assets (quoted in Aaronovitch, 1981, p. 7).

As Sir Arthur Knight, Chairman of the National Enterprise
Board and formerly of Courtaulds, has reminded us:

> It is too often forgotten that 80 per cent of our manufactur-
> ing industry is run by 400 firms, in each of which three or
> four people are responsible for the key strategic decisions
> - say 1500 at most. And in the investing industry (pension
> funds, insurance companies, etc.) I would guess that the
> number of key individuals is even smaller. (Quoted in
> Cripps et al., 1981)

The 'institutionalisation' of personal wealth in recent years
has therefore brought with it an increased concentration of
power and not, as might have been expected, a democratisation
of wealth. 'Popular' wealth has certainly grown, but the control
of that wealth has been transferred to the individuals who
administer and control it. Meanwhile, those forms of personal
wealth that continue to confer power on those who own them
remain heavily concentrated.

This vital link between wealth and power helps us, in turn,
to explain the persistence of wealth inequalities. At the outset
we suggested that this was due to the circular and self-perpetuating nature of wealth. Those who have wealth have not only

the income and the opportunity to generate and replenish their wealth-holding, but also the power with which to defend their position from challenge. Only when we have grasped the interlocking nature of wealth and power can we understand the persistence of both.

ACCUMULATION AND INHERITANCE

Some may argue that this association between wealth and power presents no cause for alarm. There is an enduring belief that differences in wealth represent differences in individual attributes and abilities. The wealthy may enjoy more of the fruits of society; but they have also contributed more to their propogation. The argument was put most forcefully by William Sumner, the prominent American economist, writing towards the end of the last century. He explained:

> The millionaires are a product of natural selection ... It is because they are thus selected that wealth - both their own and that entrusted to them - aggregates under their hands ... They may be fairly regarded as the naturally selected agents of society for certain work. They get high wages and live in luxury, but the bargain is a good one for society. (Quoted in Galbraith, 1977, p. 46)

Such crude 'Social Darwinism' is rarely expressed nowadays. In its place an elaborate body of economic theory has developed to provide justification and legitimisation for the rewards of the rich. The belief that wealth and ability go hand in hand retains a powerful grasp on the public imagination. Now if such a belief is justified, we need not concern ourselves that power is vested in the wealthy; we are in good hands. We must choose our rulers somehow; how better than to leave the choice to 'natural' or 'economic' selection.

Of course, it takes little more than simple observation to shake us out of this cosy mythology. As Robert Heller, financial journalist with 'Management Today', has explained:

> It is often only when the rich man has been incautious that the private and public images suddenly coincide and the realities emerge - that riches and true achievement bear only a tenuous relationship to each other: but that, if only you are rich enough, nobody will ever notice the truth. (Heller, 1974, p. ii)

Some of the rich, of course, are people of outstanding ability; so, as history reminds us, are some of the poor. But there is no systematic relationship. We need to look more closely, then, at the sources of wealth. We have already examined the factors influencing the change in relative shares of the rich, but we

still need to know how different groups acquired their wealth
in the first place. There is fairly general agreement that, luck
and fortune aside, people's wealth-holdings are attributable to
two main factors: inheritance and accumulation out of savings.
Accumulation itself depends, of course, on age as well as the
level of an individual's income. The relative importance attributed to each of these factors varies greatly. 'The Times', for
instance, has argued that:

> in the most egalitarian of societies one would not expect the
> new born babe and the man on the point of retirement to
> have identical savings ... and there must therefore be a
> concentration of wealth in a minority of hands in any society
> one can conceive of. Where inheritance is not allowed, only
> the old can be rich. ('The Times', September 1968 quoted in
> A.B. Atkinson, 1972)

There is clearly considerable validity in this explanation.
Those who have been continuously employed for several years
obviously have more of an opportunity to accumulate wealth
than those who have just left school. But age is not the only
factor. A preliminary examination of wealth-holdings by age,
by the Royal Commission, though subject to some deficiencies,
suggested that 'the distribution of wealth within age groups
was generally similar to that of the population as a whole'.
(Royal Commission Report No. 7, 1979, p. 96). Also important
are differences in the level of earnings from which different
groups have to save: inequalities in wealth reflect in part the
inequalities in incomes, and vice versa.
   One way of taking account of this is to build a 'model' of the
amount that people could save during their lifetime, using different assumptions about earnings and savings. Some results
from this type of exercise are in Frank Field's introductory
essay.
   Table I.1 uses data for 1974. In that year, the top 1 per cent
of wealth-holders owned 22.5 per cent of all the personal wealth.
How much of that could be explained by savings over the life-
cycle? The answer depends on the assumptions used, but the
models would lead us to expect this group to have only between
3 and 7 per cent of the total, if their wealth was accumulated
during their lifetime. Savings help to explain a larger proportion of the share of the next richest group, the top 2-5 per
cent, but it still accounts for only one-half to two-thirds of
their actual share. At the other end of the scale, the savings
of the bottom 80 per cent would have been rewarded with a
rather larger share of total wealth than was actually the case.
Thrift and hard work may put you on the road to wealth, but it
will not take you very far along it. The extremes of the distribution cannot adequately be explained by savings out of
earnings. Where, then, do the very rich acquire their wealth?
There are three other main possibilities: financial windfalls,

entrepreneurial fortunes or inheritances. The Royal Commission calculated that approximately 40 per cent of all wealth was derived from these sources. But they accounted for three-quarters of the wealth of the top 1 per cent and for over half of that of the rest of the top 5 per cent. Their importance diminished with size of the total wealth-holding. Inheritances and entrepreneurial fortunes do not fall randomly. The Royal Commission noted: 'a marked tendency for transmitted wealth and entrepreneurial fortunes to be concentrated heavily amongst the top wealth groups' (Royal Commission Report no. 7, 1979, p. 98).

A more comprehensive picture of the pattern of inheritance has been provided by work carried out by Professor Colin Harbury and David Hitchens. They undertook the laborious, but rewarding, exercise of tracing the transmission of wealth from one branch of the family tree to the next, adapting the method used by Josiah Wedgewood as long ago as 1929. The researchers examined the wealth which had been left by the fathers of the very rich - the top 0.1 per cent who owned about one-sixth of all personal wealth. These people left the equivalent (at today's prices) of about £500,000. Of these, about half the men and three-quarters of the women had fathers who left more than the equivalent of £250,000. At a compound annual rate of interest of 7 per cent, this sum might be expected to double (to the amount left by the heirs themselves) in just a decade. Three-fifths of the rich men and three-quarters of the rich women (those who left £500,000) had fathers who had left the equivalent of £125,000. Compound interest of 7 per cent would have converted that sum into £500,000 (the amount the heirs were worth) in just twenty years.

Harbury and Hitchens put the importance of inheritance into perspective by pointing out that, if there was no systematic relationship between the wealth of fathers and sons - if, for instance, inheritance was prevented by taxation or other means - it would be a matter of chance whether one had a rich father or not. In this lottery of wealth, the probability of having a rich father (worth more than £250,000) is less than one per cent. As we have seen, the odds were rather better for some people: rich men had a fifty-fifty chance of having had rich fathers; rich women had a better than even chance (3:1). The authors concluded that 'without question, the firmest conclusion to emerge from this study is that inheritance is the major determinant of wealth inequality' (Harbury and Hitchens, 1980, p. 239).

What also becomes clear from this type of analysis is the link between accumulation and inheritance. The inheritance of a substantial sum makes it very much easier to accumulate more. As Robert Heller explained to those aspiring to wealth 'time and the magic of compound interest' can help to turn even a modest inheritance into a substantial estate:

It has never been especially difficult to achieve 7 per cent
growth tax-free, which doubles your money every ten
years. ... And in half a century turns that million into
32 millions. You have to be especially inspired in your
choice of investment or adviser (and remember with a
million you can afford advice) to do worse, although it is
not impossible. (Heller, 1974, pp. 15-16)

There are many tales of self-made men and women who have
travelled the journey from rags to riches. But what makes such
stories worth the telling is that their subjects are the excep-
tions, not the rule. Many people have acquired for themselves
a comfortable enough standard of living through their own
efforts, but they are rarely to be found amongst the very
wealthy. It is inheritance that generates and perpetuates the
largest concentrations of wealth and power. It is against this
background that we should examine the operation of Britain's
system of wealth taxation. Why, contrary to all expectations,
has it had such little impact?

WEALTH TAXES IN BRITAIN

The first question we have to ask is 'why tax wealth at all?'.
Such a question may seem out of place to some who have found
the extreme inequalities outlined earlier in this chapter unacceptable, if not obscene. But the question has to be put.
The Conservative Party before it came to office had stated its
view that: 'The main pressure for heavy capital taxes has
always been political - in part mere egalitarian envy, in part a
mistaken belief that some significant redistribution of wealth
could thus be achieved to the advantage of the poor' (Conservative Party, 1976).
    On attaining office, the Conservatives set about dismantling
the system of personal wealth taxation in Britain. So the question does need to be answered, not only because there are
many who repudiate the need for any wealth taxation at all, but
also because the type of changes we propose will depend on the
objectives we want our tax system to achieve.
    The case for the effective taxation of wealth falls into three
main parts: the need to improve fairness in taxation, arguments
concerned with economic efficiency and those concerned with a
reduction in inequalities. We will consider each of these in turn.
    Arguments about fairness in taxation hinge on the principle
that the tax system should relate tax liability to ability to pay,
and that those with the same 'taxable capacity' should be taxed
in the same way. As the Chancellor of the Exchequer, Mr Healey,
pointed out in his foreword to the 'Wealth Tax' Green Paper
published in 1975: 'The ownership of wealth, whether it produces income or not, adds to the economic resources of the
taxpayer so that a person who has wealth as well as income

of a given size necessarily has a greater taxable capacity than one who has only income of that size' (Treasury, 1975).

The argument for taxation of wealth may therefore be expressed purely in terms of equity in taxation (the equal treatment of equals) without even beginning to consider questions of equality. Indeed, the Meade Committee on Tax Reform went one stage further. They argued that, since income from wealth was not subject to the same uncertainties as earned incomes, did not require expenditure of either time or work expenses by the recipient, and did not decline with age, it should be more heavily taxed than earnings. They also argued that wealth derived from inheritance should be more heavily taxed than that accumulated by the wealth-holder through his or her own efforts. (Meade, 1978, p. 350)

There is also a purely practical argument: if you tax income but not wealth, there will be a great temptation for people to switch their resources from one to the other in order to minimise their tax burden. And since the opportunities for this type of activity varies according to the level of income or wealth, the effect can be to reduce considerably the progressiveness of the income tax system.

The second plank of the case for wealth taxation rests on arguments of economic efficiency. Readers may find this surprising, since opponents of wealth taxation are fond of pointing an accusing finger towards the supposed economic costs of trying to tackle inequalities. However, the disincentive effects of taxes on capital are much less than those on income. The present Chancellor, Sir Geoffrey Howe, has justified cuts in capital taxes on the ground that such taxes are a 'severe discouragement to those seeking to build up a business and pass it on to the next generation' (Howe, 1980). This argument is based on no empirical evidence (Kay and King, 1980, p. 169). Few people wishing to start a small firm would find it much discouragement to know that, in thirty, forty or fifty years time a future Chancellor (whose name they have not yet heard) may prevent them passing the whole lot on to an heir. More immediate concerns, including survival in business, dominate the thoughts of the small-firm proprietor. Most people, of course, accumulate savings to provide security for retirement, or for future expenditure. They have little thought of passing it on. If taxation reduces the net return on that saving, some may put less aside but others will attempt to save still more to ensure they achieve their objectives.

Those who set out to accumulate wealth have a number of motives: security, power, enjoyment. Few of these are sensitive to the imposition of taxation. On the other hand, if governments raise less tax from wealth they must (for any given level of revenue) raise more from income tax. On balance, the disincentive effects are likely to be much greater.

Whatever the arguments about the effect of taxation on the incentive to accumulate wealth, it is clear that few people will

be discouraged from inheriting it, should the opportunity arise.
Once more, there is a case for the heavier taxation of inherited
than accumulated wealth.

There is a strong case for taxing wealth in terms of both tax
equity and economic efficiency, even if governments are not
particularly concerned about the extremes in wealth inequalities.
But if the aim is to achieve a fairer distribution of wealth, and
of the power which accompanies it, inherited wealth - for this
reason too - should be subject to heavier impositions of tax.
For it is the system of inheritance which serves to generate and
perpetuate the greatest inequalities.

For all these reasons, but mainly because of arguments of
economic efficiency and tax equity, several other advanced
industrial countries have annual wealth taxes. That is to say
that wealth is subject to tax each year on a set proportion of
its capital value. No such tax exists in Britain, although the
Labour Party has long been committed to an annual wealth tax.
In 1974, the Labour government even got as far as producing a
Green Paper on the subject. But by 1976 the Chancellor
announced that the proposal had been dropped and, despite
attempts by the TUC to reinstate it, the wealth tax was never
introduced (see Sandford, 1979).

Instead, wealth is taxed in three different ways in Britain:
when it changes hands; when it increases in value; and when
it yields an income. We will examine each of these in turn.

The main form of tax on wealth has throughout this century
been estate duty, introduced by Harcourt in 1894. Harcourt's
budget speech marks the birth of progressive taxation in
Britain, and he based his new tax on inherited wealth on the
argument that:

> Nature gives man no power over his earthly goods beyond
> the term of his life. What power he possesses to prolong his
> will after death - the right of a dead hand to dispose of his
> property - is a pure creation of the law, and the State has
> the right to prescribe the conditions and limitations under
> which that power shall be exercised. (quoted in Crosland,
> 1967, pp. 230-1)

Radical though Harcourt's initiative was, the new tax was
modest by present-day standards. The top rate of tax, on
estates valued at more than a million pounds, was set at 8 per
cent. Over the next 80 years, however, the top rates of tax
were gradually raised to ten times this level. It is perhaps
surprising, therefore, that the tax has not had a more marked
effect on the distribution of wealth.

When first introduced, the estate duty contributed almost
one-fifth of total direct tax receipts, and its contribution to
total tax revenue was significant throughout most of the pre-
war period. The years after the Second World War, however,
saw a consistent decline in the proportionate revenue yield,

from 9 per cent in 1948-9, to 6 per cent twenty years later and
to less than 2½ per cent in 1974-5.

Part of the explanation for this decline in revenue might be
that the share of personal wealth owned by the top groups - the
only ones liable to the tax - had declined. As we have seen,
that decline was confined to the richest 1 per cent and was less
than dramatic. The decline in revenue might also be partly
explained by an increase in institutional wealth, but even this is
insufficient explanation for the rate of decline observed. Professor Atkinson (1972) has calculated that in 1927, when the
top nominal rate stood at about 30 per cent, death duties
represented 0.42 per cent of all personal wealth holdings. By
1978 the top rate of tax had increased to 75 per cent; but the
revenue yield represented less than 0.1 per cent of personal
wealth. In other words, if the richest 1 per cent of wealth-
holders paid *all* the inheritance taxes levied, their share of
wealth (22 per cent) would fall by only a tenth of 1 per cent.
Given how small is the revenue, it is perhaps unsurprising that
the estate duties failed to fulfil Harcourt's original aspirations
of tackling wealth inequalities.

We can, of course, look at this decline in the revenue relative
to personal wealth in another way. Supposing that in 1978
estate duties (or Capital Transfer Tax as it had by then become)
raised revenue equivalent to the same relatively modest proportion of wealth as was the case fifty years before. Then we would
have expected the tax to raise about £1680 million in that year
- approximately four times the amount actually collected.

We have to look elsewhere for an explanation of the decline
in revenue from estate duty, and the most plausible explanation
is that it reflected increasing avoidance and evasion. The tax
was always comparatively simple to avoid. Being levied at death,
the taxpayer merely had to ensure that he 'passed on his wealth
before passing on himself'. The way that this practice manifest
itself in the wealth statistics was discussed earlier. Estate duty
came to be known as a form of 'optional' or 'voluntary' taxation.

The introduction of Capital Transfer Tax in 1975 was intended
to close this major loophole by including lifetime gifts in the
tax base. But whereas the CTT closed some of the options for
evasion, it provided generous exemptions. In 1981-2 the marginal
rates of tax, on gifts and bequests range from 15 per cent on
gifts valued at £50-60,000 to 50 per cent on gifts over £2 million.

The rates of tax can hardly be described as confiscatory.
Fifty thousand pounds can be given away tax free and gifts of
up to half a million pounds will still incur a top rate of tax of
only 35 per cent (little more than the standard rate of income
tax). These used to represent lifetime exemptions, but as a
result of a change in the 1981 budget (which cut substantially
the rates of tax on the largest estates) the slate can now be
wiped clean every ten years. This means that, over a period of
thirty years £150,000 can be passed on tax-free. In addition,
each person can pass on up to £3,000 each year tax free. Over

a period of thirty years, therefore, a wealthy couple could
pass on the equivalent of a third of a million pounds without
paying a penny in tax. As a result of the changes in the 1981
budget especially, Capital Transfer Tax has now virtually been
abolished (Low Pay Unit, 1981).

Capital Transfer Tax is the main form of wealth tax in Britain
but it is not the only one. Capital Gains Tax and the investment income surcharge are both forms of tax on the income
from wealth. Table 1.3 shows what has happened to the revenue
yield of all three in recent years.

Sir Geoffrey Howe has spoken of 'the rising yield of capital
taxes as a result of inflation'. The figures show a different
story. Over the period 1973-4 to 1981-2 income tax receipts
quadrupled, from just over £7 billion to an estimated £28 billion.
Capital Transfer Tax revenue remained roughly constant in
money terms. Its contribution to total revenue has fallen from
4p in every pound collected to little more than 1p in the pound.

The same picture emerges from the other forms of capital
taxes. Investment income surcharge is intended to discriminate
in favour of earned incomes, for the reasons described by the
Meade Committee and referred to above. Hence, investment
incomes of more than £5500 (after allowances and reliefs) were
subject to a surcharge on the normal income tax rates of 15
per cent. However, earned incomes are also subject to a surcharge - the national insurance contributions - from which
investment incomes are exempt. This means that investment
incomes below £5500 are taxed at a rate of only 30p in the
pound, while earnings below this level are subject to a marginal
rate of tax (in 1981-2) of $37\frac{3}{4}$p in the pound.

The average male might have expected to earn about £8,000
a year in 1981. If he paid tax on this as earnings he would
have £2,376.50 (29.7 per cent) deducted. If he received the
same amount as investment income, he would pay tax of only
£1,809.75 (22.6 per cent). Income from wealth is less heavily
taxed than income from employment.

This is only 'productive' wealth, i.e. wealth that yields an
income. Under the British arrangements such wealth is liable
to a modest rate of tax. But unproductive wealth - yachts, cars
and houses, for instance - are still more favourably treated.
Take the example of the new Silver Spirit Rolls-Royce announced
in 1980. One might generally think the cost of £50,000 a pro-
hibitively large amount to spend on a motor car. The Inland
Revenue is, however, willing to help out. Suppose the alternative were to invest the same amount in manufacturing stock,
offering an interest of 10 per cent (a not unreasonable rate of
return on such stock in 1980). The gross annual income from
that investment would be £5,000 a year, but tax would be payable on that sum. Indeed, someone paying tax at the highest
rate on investment income would be left with only £1,250. Since
this is less than the cost of a second-hand mini, the wealth-
holder may be tempted to buy the Rolls-Royce instead.

TABLE 1.3 *Contribution of capital taxes to total Inland Revenue receipts 1973-4 – 1981-2*

	Estate duty/ Capital Transfer Tax		Capital Gains Tax		Investment Income Surcharge		All Capital Taxes[b]	
	£m	%	£m	%	£m	%	£m	%
1973-4	412	3.9	324	3.0	136	1.3	872	8.2
1974-5	339	2.4	382	2.7	202	1.4	923	6.5
1975-6	330	1.8	387	2.1	232	1.3	949	5.2
1976-7	383	1.8	323	1.6	265	1.3	971	4.2
1977-8	398	1.8	340	1.6	253	1.2	991	4.5
1978-9	369	1.5	353	1.6	(313)	(1.3)*	1035	4.3[a]
1979-80	430	1.5	410	1.5	(365)	(1.3)*	1205	4.3[a]
1980-1	442	1.3	520	1.6	(434)	(1.3)*	1396	4.2[a]
1981-2[c]	460	1.2	575	1.5	(508)	(1.3)*	1543	3.9[a]

Notes: a. Estimated on the assumption that Investment Income Surcharge continues to raise 1.3% of all Inland Revenue Receipts. b. Excluding Stamp Duties and Development Land Tax (DLT). c. Treasury forecasts.
Source: C. Pond (1980), updated by 'Financial Statement and Budget Report', London, HMSO, March 1981.

The Investment Income Surcharge is not the only form of tax on the income from wealth. Wealth may provide an income in the form of rents, interest or dividends (taxed under the Investment Income Surcharge IIS) or as a capital gain when the asset is sold. Capital gains are rarely taxed (see Chapter 2) and even when they are, the rate is a flat 30p in the pound on gains of more than £3,000 a year. Capital Gains Tax has been described by Sir Geoffrey Howe as 'a capricious and sometimes savage levy'. A quick reference back to Table 1.3 will confirm that this is much like accusing a rabbit of terrorising a neighbourhood. Even in cash terms, CTT revenue has increased little since 1973-4. Its contribution to total revenue has halved. Moreover, Capital Gains Tax is much less harsh than income tax on earned income. To return to an example of someone receiving £8,000, we showed that this sum would attract less tax as an investment income than as earnings; it would attract still less as a capital gain. The maximum tax payable would be £1,500 (18.8 per cent) - less than two-thirds of the amount paid by a wage-earner with the same income.

To see Capital Gains Tax in operation, let us return to our taxpayer mulling over the difficult decision of how to spend £50,000. If he buys the Rolls-Royce he will apparently lose a net income of £1,250. But, of course, his accountant might explain, the Rolls-Royce will probably go up in value. He may be able to sell it for more than he bought it for. Since private cars are exempt from CGT he would pay no tax at all on this gain, but even if he decided to invest in other assets which, while yielding no income would rise in value, his maximum tax liability would be 30p in the pound.

This clearly is attractive to taxpayers who might otherwise be subject to the investment income surcharge of up to 75p in the pound; tax liability can be reduced substantially if investment incomes can be converted into capital gains. In this, once more, the government is helpful, by issuing certain types of gilt-edged stock which yield a low rate of interest (subject to investment income surcharge) but promise a good capital gain, which in this case is tax free. Kay and King (1980) have estimated that 'at least £3000 million is invested in Government stocks which are clearly unattractive to anyone who is not a higher rate taxpayer' (p. 45). Capital Gains Tax should therefore be considered less of a tax, and more a tax-avoidance device. It probably has a much greater effect in increasing inequalities in income, by reducing the progressiveness of the income tax system, than in reducing inequalities in wealth.

The capital tax system in Britain is now virtually non-existent. For fewer people paid the investment income surcharge in 1978-9 than had been the case in 1974-5, while the revenue from CTT and CGT has barely increased even in cash terms since 1973-4. Capital taxes as a whole contribute less than 4p in every pound raised in direct taxes - half as much as in 1973-4. Sam Brittan, an economist who generally supports the

Conservative government's approach, once wrote: 'Is it conceivable that if a new [tax] system were being designed for
Britain that income would be taxed so heavily and effectively,
and capital hardly at all?' (Brittan, 1964).
When these words were written in the early 1960s, the burden
of capital taxation was far higher than it is today. Yet the
present Conservative government persists with the myth that
capital taxes are 'oppressive'. As we have seen, they have
virtually eliminated CTT in just two years, and have threatened
to abolish altogether the investment income surcharge and
Capital Gains Tax. To do so would widen wealth inequalities
still further and increase the burden on income tax.
    In 1980, 'Financial Weekly', not the most radical of papers,
warned the government against further cuts in capital taxes:

At the moment when the Chancellor is telling the nation that it
must carry on with its strict monetarist diet of bread and
water ... he would be announcing that the very wealthiest
section of it could not merely carry on eating its cake, but
have a dollop of cream on top as well.

And the article went on to warn:

the uproar would surely not be confined to the left. Con-
servatives are not deeply devoted to equality, but neither
- unless they have entirely forgotten the principles of
Disraeli - are they deeply devoted to widening social
divisions. And Conservative MPs undoubtedly number
more of the unemployed and of the low paid among their
constituents and indeed voters than they do payers of
these capital taxes. ('Financial Weekly', 1980)

Whether the government heeds this advice remains to be seen.
    The present government is clearly not in favour of reductions
in wealth inequalities. Their changes in capital taxation,
combined with the abolition of exchange controls, have tended
to work in the opposite direction. The Labour Party is committed to tackling these inequalities and to using a wealth tax
as the central plank of that policy. However, the Labour Party's
proposals have not, in the past, been well developed and have
therefore collapsed in the face of inevitable resistance (see
Sandford, 1979). How might a future government set about
implementing radical tax reform? In our view, it is important
to bear in mind objectives of economic efficiency and equity in
taxation, as well as that of reducing inequality.
    Since inheritance is the main driving force of wealth inequali-
ties, the central pivot of a radical tax policy must be an inheritance tax. The present Capital Transfer Tax, like its predeces-
sor, death duties, is a tax on the dead rather than the living
(Wainwright, 1981). Tax is assessed, under a progressive
schedule on the total amount given away by any one individual

over a period of ten years. It does not matter whether he gives
it all to one person or spreads his generosity widely. It encour-
ages continued concentration of wealth. Nor does it matter if
the recipient is already a millionaire from another source or
whether he is penniless. The tax payable will be the same.
The tax should be what has come to be known as an 'accession
tax', payable at progressive rates on all gifts or inheritances
received, from whatever source, during the recipient's life
(Sandford et al., 1973). The exemptions against tax should
be much lower than now, and the rates should rise steeply,
perhaps to 100 per cent at some level.

Such a tax would do a great deal, over time, to reduce
inequalities. It would do this both by encouraging the wealthy
to spread their wealth more widely and by imposing effective
taxes on transfers. The effect may not, however, be seen for
many generations (since tax would only apply when wealth
changed hands). Nor would it overcome the economic inef-
ficiencies or inequity between taxpayers of the current system.
There is a need for an annual wealth tax, perhaps combined
with the accessions tax as the Meade Committee have proposed.

This would mean that when a person received a sum of
wealth he would pay not only an inheritance tax but a tax to
represent an annual levy on the wealth over the period he was
expected to hold that wealth. If he disposed of the wealth
sooner than expected a rebate would be payable. Once again,
the wider dispersion of wealth would be encouraged (Meade,
1978).

In addition to this capital levy element of the accessions tax,
there is a need for a separate annual wealth tax payable on all
wealth, whether accumulated or inherited. The rates of tax
would depend on the purpose of the tax; but if it was intended
to contribute to a reduction in wealth inequalities, the rate
payable on the largest wealth-holdings would have to be high
enough to offset the net income earned on that wealth. If the
tax were merely paid out of the annual income from the wealth,
the largest wealth-holdings would remain intact, or even grow
in size.

These proposals are concerned with the capital value of wealth.
They would ensure that inherited wealth would be taxed more
heavily than that accumulated out of savings, and would encourage the wider dispersion of wealth. But we still need to deal with
the income from wealth. In our view, the best approach would
be to adopt a Comprehensive Income Tax (CIT) which taxed all
income, no matter what its source, under the same progressive
schedule of rates. Whether the income was in the form of
earnings or capital gains, fringe benefits or investment incomes,
tax would be applied in the same way. This would reduce the
opportunities for tax avoidance and remove the incentive for
taxpayers to distort their affairs by switching their income from
one source to another. Economic efficiency, as well as equality,
would be improved.

There remains the question of national insurance contributions,
which currently operate as an 'earned income surcharge', dis-
criminating in favour of the owners of capital. In our view these
should be abolished as a separate, and regressive, social
security 'tax'. The revenue required to finance social security
would be raised through the Comprehensive Income Tax together with a social security 'payroll' tax on employers. This
would, of course, mean that capital, as well as earnings, would
be required to make a contribution to the costs of social security.
It would also mean that the insurance principle on which the
present system of income maintainence is theoretically based
would be abandoned. This is already largely the case in practice. Benefits paid are not properly related to contributions,
and the contributions are not calculated on true actuarial
principles. Working people have paid a high price (through the
regressive contribution scheme) for the largely mythical
insurance principle. Contributions should be related to ability
to pay and benefits according to need. (For a more detailed
discussion of such proposals, see Pond and MacLennan, 1981.)
    Wealth tax changes since the war have had little impact on the
distribution of wealth. The inequalities are almost as great as
they were half a century ago. A radical and comprehensive
tax policy of the type outlined above is necessary if we are to
break into the otherwise self-perpetuating cycle of wealth,
power and privilege which still scars our society.

NOTE

*This chapter owes a great deal to Louie Burghes, from whose
work and advice I have benefited greatly. I am grateful to her
and Bill Smith for allowing me to draw on an earlier joint
pamphlet ('Taxing Wealth Inequalities', Fabian Society, 1980).
Emma MacLennan, Clive Playford and Lesley Day commented
on an earlier draft of the paper which Jill Sullivan prepared for
the publishers. Errors that remain are mine alone.

The right to be unequal: inequality in incomes

Clive Playford and Chris Pond

Post-war governments, almost without exception, have held as
one of their objectives the attainment of a 'fairer' or more equal
society. Sometimes this commitment has been more implicit than
explicit; sometimes it has not had very high priority. But it has
always been there. The advent of the Conservative government
in 1979 marked a sharp severing of that consensus. Mrs Thatcher
herself had declared a commitment to a rather different doctrine
as early as 1975: 'The pursuit of equality is a mirage. What is
more desirable and more practical than the pursuit of equality
is the pursuit of equality of opportunity. And opportunity
means nothing unless it includes the right to be unequal' (quoted
in 'Labour Research', 1976, p. 171). By a masterly suspense of
logic, the future Prime Minister was able to demonstrate, to her
own satisfaction at least, that inequality and equality of opportunity were one and the same thing. Inequality was now to be
a positive goal of government. And just as the promise to make
Britain a fairer society had previously been judged as an
electoral asset, 1979 saw the election of a government committed
to an increase in inequality.

This change reflected an assumption that the previous thirty
years had witnessed a substantial movement towards equality of
incomes. Indeed, even Labour governments of the late 1960s
and 1970s had begun to express concern that this movement
had progressed so far that traditional differentials were beginning to break down, and with them the incentives that are the
driving force of a market economy.

In this chapter we examine the validity of this assumption. In
the first part of the chapter we examine the official evidence on
changes in the distribution of incomes since 1949. We then
consider some of the modifications necessary to conclusions
about the magnitude of income inequalities given the known
deficiencies in the official statistics. Official data on the overall

34

distribution are, in any case, only available up to 1977-8. In the final part of the chapter, therefore, we assess the information available on the different components of income to try and piece together a picture of the more recent changes.

WEALTH AND INCOMES

In the last chapter we examined the distribution of wealth. Here we turn our attention to the distribution of incomes. 'Wealth' was treated as a snapshot of the stock of assets owned by an individual at a given point in time. 'Income' is treated as a flow of resources between two points in time; weekly wages, monthly salary, annual bonus and so on.

Such a distinction is, of course, highly artificial. Income and wealth are merely different ways of expressing an individual's command over economic resources. And each feeds into the other. Wealth earns for its owner an income in the form of interest, rents, dividends or capital gains which, if saved, helps to replenish or build on the stock of wealth. Those with large holdings of wealth are likely to enjoy a high income from it, while those with a high income have a better chance of making it into the selected elite of top wealth-holders.

Ideally, an assessment of the true level of economic inequality would require a measure which combines all the resources available to individuals or families. The Royal Commission on the Distribution of Income and Wealth recognised that 'the judgement of inequality may depend not only on separate analysis of income and wealth but also on the understanding of the links between them' (Royal Commission Report No. 7, 1979, p. 11). They examined the possibility of devising a combined measure, either by converting all future income flows to their capitalised value at a point in time (converting all income into 'wealth') or by calculating the annuity values of wealth to convert all wealth into incomes. They concluded that such an exercise was beyond the bounds of practicality at present, although they signalled their intention to calculate a 'joint distribution' of income and wealth as part of their future work programme. Unfortunately, the advent of a Conservative administration spelt the demise of the Commission before this task could be executed.

Recently, however, Peter Townsend has attempted to merge the two concepts of income and wealth into a single measure (based on the annuity value of assets together with net disposable incomes) to provide a measure of 'income net worth'. The results showed, as might be expected, that the distribution was less equal than that measured solely in terms of net disposable incomes, and Professor Townsend concluded that: 'the distinction so often made between "flow" and "stock", revenue and capital, or income and wealth, tends to lead society to underestimate the scale of inequality' (Townsend, 1979, p. 230). Unfortunately, Professor Townsend's data related to the late

1960s and no analyses over time, before or since that date, are yet available. We must therefore content ourselves with an examination of the inequality of income separate from that of wealth, always maintaining a keen awareness of the artificiality of such a distinction.

THE DISTRIBUTION OF INCOME

There is a growing literature on how inaccurate the official statistics on income distribution are (Royal Commission Report No. 1 (1975) and Report No. 7 (1979)). Three sources of data are published: The Survey of Personal Incomes (SPI), the Family Expenditure Survey (FES), and a combination of the two which goes under the title of the Blue Book data. This last is the most accurate of the three, but even here this carefully nurtured offspring appears to have inherited some of the weaker characteristics of its parents. While the Blue Book figures include certain elements of non-taxable income (those below the exemption limit and short-term benefits), those elements rendered 'non-taxable' by avoidance and evasion are still missing. The problem of 'part-year incomes' remains, tending to overstate the number on low incomes. And no allowance is made for differences in need: a single person and a married couple with three children are both recorded as single 'tax units'. This can be very important. Investment incomes, capital gains, fringe benefits and self-employment incomes are all under-recorded with the result that the official statistics, even when adjusted by the Central Statistical Office (CSO), similarly understate the true level of economic inequality. First, we consider the evidence on income distribution as supplied in the CSO Blue Book data. We should bear this in mind when considering the degree of inequality and the changes that have taken place during the post-war period. We will consider the likely impact of these shortcomings in the data later in the chapter.

It is generally assumed that the post-war period has witnessed a substantial movement towards equality in incomes. The statistics present a rather different picture. Certainly, the share of the top 1 per cent has halved since 1949, from 11 per cent of the total to $5\frac{1}{2}$ per cent. The remainder of the top 5 per cent have suffered a much smaller decline in their share, (from $12\frac{1}{2}$ to $10^{3}/_{4}$ per cent) while the next richest 5 per cent have slightly improved their position. Overall, the richest 10 per cent had one-third of the incomes in 1949, compared with slightly more than a quarter in 1978-9. But, as with changes in the distribution of wealth, the decline in income shares has been confined to the top 5 per cent.

As the Royal Commission noted:

These changes at the top were not reflected in substantial increases in the share of income accruing to the lowest income units. In 1949, the income share of those in the bottom half of the distribution was 23.7 per cent and, although this had increased slightly by 1976-7 they still had less than a quarter of total income. In contrast, the income share of those in the top half of the distribution but below the top ten per cent, increased by more than six percentage points.... The overall impression from the figures is of a reduction in inequality but, if the decline in the share of the top one per cent is ignored, the shape of the distribution is not greatly different in 1976-7 to what it was in 1949. The major part of the fall in the share of the top one per cent is balanced by an increase in the shares of other groups in the top half of the distribution. (Royal Commission Report No. 7, 1979, p. 17)

Changes in the distribution of income during the post-war years have been much less dramatic than is generally assumed, even on the basis of the Blue Book statistics which, as we argue below, may overstate the actual decline. Where does that leave us today?

We should remember that after 1975-6 the figures were adjusted to include deductions such as mortgage interest relief, pensions, etc. This adjustment showed the degree of inequality to be greater still. The latest information, for 1978-9, includes those elements. The degree of inequality in incomes is by no means as pronounced as that of wealth; but it is still substantial. The richest 1 per cent, having average incomes in 1978-9 of almost £22,000 a year, had a larger share of the total income than the poorest fifth of the population between them. The richest 10 per cent (average incomes almost £11,000) had a larger share than half the population (26.1 per cent compared with 23.5 per cent) and ten times as much as the poorest tenth.

These figures include earned and unearned incomes combined, although they understate the importance of unearned income. The degree of inequality in the latter is brought into sharp relief if we separate these two elements. Using reworked Royal Commission data, Frank Field (1981, p. 157) demonstrates that income from wealth is even more unequally distributed than wealth itself. This is demonstrated in Table 2.1, which relates to 1975-6. As we noted earlier in this chapter, inequality in wealth reflects itself in inequality in incomes. While the top 1 per cent received about 5 per cent of the earned incomes, they enjoyed almost 30 per cent of the unearned incomes. The top 10 per cent received a quarter of the earned incomes, but more than half of the unearned.

Comparing these figures with those on the distribution of wealth in the last chapter, it will be seen that, while earned incomes are more equally divided than wealth, unearned incomes are less equally shared. We noted, for instance, that 1 per cent

of the population received about 24 per cent of the wealth; but
1 per cent of unearned income recipients received 28 per cent
of the income from wealth. As Atkinson has suggested, this
may be because the very wealthy receive a higher return on
their assets than those with modest wealth-holdings (1972,
p. 37).

TABLE 2.1 *The distribution of income from wealth, 1975-6*

Income group	Share of earned income	Share of unearned income	Share of all income
Top 1 per cent	4.8	27.6	6.0
Top 10 per cent	25.8	55.0	27.3
Top 20 per cent	42.8	64.8	43.9
Top 50 per cent	77.7	84.9	78.1
Bottom 10 per cent	2.2	0.9	2.1

Source: Field (1981), p. 157; reworked data.

THE EFFECTS OF TAXATION

Of course, the analysis so far has been solely in terms of pre-
tax incomes. Since the income tax system is the main instrument
available to governments wishing to modify the degree of
inequality, we should really examine what has happened to the
post-tax distribution. This is shown in Table 2.2.

The results are rather surprising. Most people would assume
that Britain's income tax system is markedly progressive, and
that it has become more so in recent years. The official statistics on income distribution tell a different story. The effect of
income tax is to reduce the share of the richest 1 per cent,
from 5.3 per cent to just under 4 per cent in 1978-9. This is a
reduction in their share of about one third, somewhat less than
might have been expected given a tax system with marginal tax
rates rising to 98p in the pound, as was the case in that year.
The share of the richest 10 per cent is affected still less. Their
share falls from 26 per cent before tax to 23 per cent after tax
– a reduction in their share of only a tenth. Most of this reduction was borne by the top 1 per cent. Meanwhile, the share of
the poorest tenth is increased from only 2.4 per cent of the
total to under 3 per cent.

We should point out that these figures reflect only the effect
of income tax, the most progressive element of the tax system.
If national insurance contributions, indirect taxes on spending
and local authority rates were included they would almost
certainly neutralise and very possibly reverse, the modest effect
of income tax on the overall degree of inequality. Even by the
mid-1970s the Royal Commission reported that 'the progressive

TABLE 2.2 *Percentage shares of income, before and after income tax, received by given quartile groups, 1949 – 1978-9*

Percentage share of	1949	1959	1970-1	1976-7 (old basis)	1976-7 (new basis)	1977-8	1978-9
Before income tax							
Top 1 per cent	11.2	8.4	6.6	5.4	5.5	5.5	5.3
Top 10 per cent	33.2	29.4	27.5	25.8	26.2	26.2	26.1
Next 40 per cent	43.1	47.5	49.0	49.7	49.7	49.8	50.4
Bottom 50 per cent	27.3	23.0	23.5	24.5	24.1	23.9	23.5
Bottom 10 per cent	–	–	2.5	2.5	2.5	2.5	2.4
After income tax							
Top 1 per cent	6.4	5.3	4.5	3.5	3.9	3.9	3.9
Top 10 per cent	27.1	25.2	23.9	22.4	23.2	23.3	23.4
Next 40 per cent	46.4	49.7	49.9	50.0	49.9	50.2	50.4
Bottom 50 per cent	26.5	25.0	26.1	27.6	26.9	26.5	26.2
Bottom 10 per cent	–	–	–	3.1	3.0	3.0	2.9

Source: Royal Commission (1977) and 'Economic Trends' (1981).

effect of direct taxation is largely offset by the regressive effect
of indirect taxation. Thus the tax system has little effect on
the overall shape of the distribution' (1975, Report No. 1,
p. 168). That statement would have still more validity today.
Remember, too, that the figures shown above are now relatively
old, relating to 1978-9. Since then we have witnessed regressive modifications to the tax system under both Labour and
Conservative governments (for details see the chapter by
Chris Pond in 'The Wealth Report' (Field, 1979c) and Chapter 3
in this volume).

Looking back over the post-war period, the tax system
appears actually to have mitigated the decline in the shares
of the top groups. As the Royal Commission remarked in its
first report, 'Post-tax changes over the period 1949 to 1972-3
were in general smaller than those in shares of income before
tax. For example, the share of the top one per cent after tax
fell by nearly one third whereas pre-tax it fell by slightly
more than two fifths' (Royal Commission Report No.1, 1975,
p. 44). This conclusion remains true looking over the slightly
longer period reflected in Table 2.2. Why should this have been
the case? The answer can be found by examining the changes in
the structure and burden of income tax over the period considered which can best be done by examining the level of
income at which a typical two-child family begins to pay income
tax. The entry point to the tax system has fallen steadily from
99.5 per cent of average earnings in 1955 to (an estimated) 38
per cent in 1981. Meanwhile, the structure of tax rates has also
changed. In the mid-1950s, the taxpayer would begin to pay
tax at a rate of only 9p in the pound, even when he entered
the tax system. There were two more reduced rates of tax
before the full 'standard' rate (of 33p in the pound) was payable on earnings of more than $1^{3}/_{4}$ times the average. The
abolition of the reduced rates of tax resulted in an increase in
the rate at which families started to pay tax, while the level of
income at which they became liable for tax fell lower year by
year. As a result of a combination of these changes, the marginal rate of tax payable by those on less than average earnings trebled over the period. That payable by those on twice
average earnings remained roughly the same, while the top
rates of tax fell over the quarter century considered here. (For
a fuller discussion, see Field, Meacher and Pond, 1977. These
changes in the structure of taxation were reflected in changes
in the overall burden of income tax. Over the period 1959 to
1976-7 the average tax burden doubled, but that of the richest
1 per cent increased by only 12 per cent, and that of the
richest 10 per cent by only 26 per cent. The proportionate tax
burden of the poorest 40 per cent increased fourfold (Royal
Commission Report No. 7, 1979, p. 30).

This meant that over the same period the relative contribution
of the rich to income tax declined: the top 1 per cent's contribution fell from 34½p in every pound collected in 1959 to just 13p

in the pound (little more than one-third as much) in 1976-7.
The contribution of the top 10 per cent fell from 65p in the
pound to only 39½p in 1976-7. This being a zero-sum game
(what the rich don't contribute, someone else must) the relative
contributions of all other groups increased. As the Royal Commission noted, 'most of the proportionate increase in income tax
collected, therefore, has been paid by individuals at lower
income levels' (Report no. 7, 1979, p.32). They went on to
explain that this change in the tax burden could not be fully
explained by changes in relative shares of income.

A MORE EQUAL BRITAIN?

Earlier in this chapter we discussed some of the shortcomings
of the official statistics on income distribution. Some of these,
particularly the inclusion of part-year incomes, had the effect
of overstating the degree of inequality. But others, such as
the under-recording of self-employment incomes, fringe benefits
and capital gains, have a powerful effect in the opposite direction. On balance CSO figures probably understate significantly
the true degree of inequality. We have seen that the inclusion
of capital gains alone can, in certain circumstances, be reflected
in a doubling in the share of the very richest individuals (Field,
1981). It may be argued, however, that although the pattern of
inequality shown for any one year may be distorted, 'it does
not follow that the *trends* of changes in income distribution ...
would be discredited' (Nicholson, 1973, p. 100). Such trends,
it is suggested, will only be distorted if the data is inconsistent,
year by year, in terms of what is included and what is left out:
we may not know how unequal the distribution of incomes now
is, but we do know that it is less unequal than was the case in
1949.
    Unfortunately, even this modest conclusion is open to doubt.
As the Royal Commission warned: 'Excluded items such as fringe
benefits or mortgage interest payments, may have been growing
at a different rate from that of other components of income, the
trends revealed, therefore, should also be treated with caution'
(Royal Commission Report No. 7, 1979, p. 24). We have seen
that the share of income received by the bottom half of income
recipients after tax increased by little more than one percentage
point between 1949 and 1976-7; the share of the richest 1 per
cent, after tax, fell by less than three percentage points. In
the last chapter we referred to the very substantial growth in
owner-occupied housing which nevertheless remained concentrated in the top half of the population. We have also seen
that the exclusion of mortgage interest deductions (until
1975-6) from the CSO statistics tended to understate the true
share of income of the richest groups. This alone could have
wiped out the small increase in the measured share of the
poorest 50 per cent or the small decrease in that of the richest

one per cent. But there were still more powerful factors at work,
in particular the growth of fringe benefits, the regressive
effects of price changes on income distribution, and the effects
of tax avoidance and evasion. We will consider each of these in
turn.

FRINGE BENEFITS

Among the many shortcomings of the official statistics on income
distribution, summarised above, the omission of the value of
fringe benefits is one of the most serious. As long ago as 1962,
Richard Titmuss warned that 'as a result of the growth of
"fringe benefits" the Blue Book figures of salaries and wages
are becoming increasingly inappropriate as a guide to income
differentials' (Titmuss, 1962). What was true then is even more
so today. The official data on incomes can only reflect fringe
benefits to the extent that they are taxable and, perhaps more
importantly, to the extent that they are declared for tax. This
leaves a severe gap in our information on income distribution.
     However, some data are available from independent sources,
which enables us to close this gap to some extent. The Table
2.3 shows how rapidly fringe benefits grew between 1974 and
1978 alone. This is particularly true of the higher managerial
positions: while fringe benefits and superannuation made up
12 per cent of the average managing director's total remuneration package in 1974, by 1978 the figure had leapt to 36 per
cent - over a third of the total packages. The biggest jump
occurred between 1974 and 1975. The Royal Commission (from
whose Report No. 7 the table is taken) warn that the figures
are subject to considerable sampling error and that this jump
may not, therefore, have been as dramatic as the table suggests.
It is clear, nevertheless, that at a time when the Labour government was attempting to reduce income inequalities by limiting
the pay increases of the better paid and increasing the higher
income tax rates, Britain's highest paid executives were success-
fully side-stepping the squeeze by taking a higher proportion
of their total remuneration in fringe benefits.
     The range of fringe benefits available is considerable. It
includes the payment of private telephone bills; private school
fees; travel and accident insurance; subsidised lunches; widow's
and dependant's pensions; private medical insurance; loans at
low interest rates; and free or subsidised housing. By far the
most popular benefits, are generous pensions (frequently non-
contributory), free life insurance, and free company car. Since
the advent of a Conservative government in May 1979, which
reduced very substantially the higher rates of income tax, the
popularity of some fringe benefits has declined. As Table 2.4
demonstrates, however, the 'big three' benefits are still as
popular as ever and certain other benefits (those which employers can purchase in bulk at a discount) are also still growing in
popularity.

TABLE 2.3 *Cost of fringe benefits and superannuation: 1974-8*

Job level	July 1974	July 1975	July 1976	July 1977	July 1978
	Cost to employer of superannuation and fringe benefits as percentage of average salary plus bonus and commission before tax.				
Superintendent	17	18	21	22	18
Works Manager	23	23	26	29	29
Manufacturing Manager	25	26	29	31	33
General Manager	16	26	29	31	37
Managing Director	12	29	33	35	36

Source: Royal Commission Report No. 7, 1979, Table 2.22, p. 53.

TABLE 2.4 *Percentage of directors and supporting managers receiving selected fringe benefits, January 1974–January 1981*

Benefit	1974 %	1980 %	1981 %
Free telephone or allowance	14.0	24.3	20.7
School fees	4.0	6.6	5.4
Private Medical Insurance	31.0	45.6	55.4
Low Interest Loans	24.0	19.0	27.0
Life Insurance	91.0[a]	94.5	96.8
Travel accident insurance	n/a	83.7	85.9
Special Service Contract	13.5	16.0	15.3

Note: a. Refers to percentage of firms providing cover rather than percentage of individuals covered.
Source: 'National management salary surveys', British Institute of Management (1974, 1980, 1981).

The proportion of executives enjoying sole use of a company car grew from 48 per cent in 1974 to 53.6 per cent in 1980. By 1981 it had fallen to 46 per cent, but most of this decline is accounted for by a marked movement at lower management levels from company cars to car allowances. At the lowest management grade in the 1981 BIM survey only 15 per cent had company cars (35 per cent in 1980), but 39 per cent had car allowances (11 per cent in 1980). The authors of the BIM report suggest that this can be explained by the fact that allowances are more attractive to employers as they are simpler, more flexible and less capital intensive than providing company cars and are 'quite possibly to the benefit of the individual from the income tax position' (BIM, 1981). Among directors, company cars continue to be an almost universal benefit, and a very

lucrative one. In January 1981 97.5 per cent of directors
enjoyed the sole use of a company car. For one in eight of
them this perk came in addition to their prime use of a
chauffeur-driven company car.

Although the 1974-9 Labour government introduced taxation of
company cars, the tax liability is minimal in relation to their real
value. According to the British Institute of Management (1979)
the most popular makes of car for directors are Rovers, Jaguars,
and Fords, with Volvos and BMWs not far behind. The majority
of directors' cars are therefore probably in the £9,601-£14,400
price range. Cars in this price range incur a tax liability of
only £660 a year, which costs the recipient a maximum of £396
in extra tax or £7.60 a week.

The real value of a company car is undoubtedly well above
this figure, however. 'Motoring Which?' calculates, for example,
that the running costs (petrol, oil, maintenance, insurance) of
a Rover 3500 amount to almost £1,500 a year, while depreciation
adds a further £3,120. Thus, even if private use accounts for
only half, say, of the total mileage, a company car is still worth
at least £2,300 a year. As only £660 of this is taxable, a company car therefore confers a tax free bonus of more than
£1,600 - equivalent to a gross salary of around £4,000 to someone in the top 60 per cent income tax bracket. Small wonder
then that the Chancellor himself had to admit in his March 1981
budget statement that company car tax scales 'fall well short of
the true value' ('Hansard', 10 March 1981, col. 774). His
decision to raise the scales by 20 per cent in April 1982 will do
little to redress the balance.

In addition to company cars, executives receive a wide range
of other benefits, the most popular of which remains free
insurance: 96.8 per cent of executives receive free life insurance and 85.9 per cent receive free travel/accident insurance.
Private medical insurance is also catching up rapidly with 55
per cent of executives covered in 1981 - 10 per cent more than
in 1980 and 24 per cent more than in 1974. The BIM survey
also reveals that executives are enjoying longer holidays than
ever. While only 22 per cent of directors and 13 per cent of
other executives received more than five weeks holiday in 1979,
the corresponding figures in 1981 were 31 per cent and 21 per
cent respectively. Moreover, almost 90 per cent of all executives
enjoyed more than four weeks holiday in 1981, proportionately
three times as many as were in this position in 1974.

RELATIVE PRICE CHANGES

The provision of a wide range of fringe benefits almost
certainly means that the official statistics regarding the distribution of income seriously underestimate the level of inequality
in incomes. It is now widely accepted that fringe benefits do
distort the statistics in this way, but it is less widely realised

that the provision of such benefits also helps to cushion the recipients from the full impact of inflation. Inflation is an important factor to be taken into account when assessing the changes that have taken place in the distribution of incomes since the war. Our analysis so far has been concerned with changes in the money incomes of different groups, before and after tax. Of course, real living standards are determined not by the amount of money received by each individual or family, but by what that money will buy. Changes in prices need to be considered when asessing real incomes.

'Inflation' tends to be treated as an objective concept. We are told that 'the inflation rate' is this percentage or that. But this is only a measure of the rate of change in prices as reflected in the official Retail Prices Index (RPI) based on an 'average' basket of goods and services. Only families whose spending mirrors exactly the pattern assessed in the RPI will experience exactly the official inflation rate. Others will find prices rising faster or slower, depending on their actual spending. For instance, an increase in the price of necessities will affect the poor more than the rich, and an increase in the retail price of yachting equipment is unlikely to cause anxiety to many poor families.

A number of commentators have tried to assess the impact of relative price changes on the degree of real income inequality since the war. Most are agreed that the effect of rent and price controls during the war and early post-war years served to reduce still further the level of inequality (Seers, 1951). Brittain (1960), for instance, found that over the period 1938 to 1946 prices rose by 66 per cent for households at the top decile, compared with only 59 per cent for those at the lower quartile. In the next ten years, however, the pattern reversed, and Brittain recorded 'substantial bias' against low income households (quoted in Muellbauer, 1978, p. 331).

A number of independent studies confirm that this differential bias in inflation against the poor continued between the mid-1950s and mid-1970s (for a summary, see Pond, 1977). Two of these have attempted to provide a consistent series over relatively long periods of time. Examining the years 1963 to 1975, Stephen Hill (1978) concluded, in his evidence to the Royal Commission:

> Over the period prices increased by 150 per cent for the lowest decile and 141 per cent for the highest decile. The differences in prices meant that the inequality of money incomes was extended when applied to real incomes in terms of constant 1963 prices ... the share of the lowest four deciles fell during 1963-1975, with the major change occurring after 1967, whilst the share of the top four deciles increased. The second decile lost most, and the ninth decile gained most, in this redistribution of real income.
> (p. 210)

An attempt to provide a consistent series over an even longer
period was made by David Piachaud (1976). His results suggested that differential inflation was particularly strong between 1956 and 1961 and again between 1971 and 1974, with
only a small bias against the poor in the intervening years.
Nevertheless, over the whole period (1956 to 1974) Piachaud
found that prices rose for the poorest 5 per cent by 26 percentage points more than for all families and by 30.9 percentage
points more than for the richest 5 per cent.

These results suggest that the small reduction in income
inequality which the official figures suggest has occurred in
cash terms since 1949, has been offset by the effects of inflation. Using Piachaud's calculations and comparing these with
FES figures on changes in gross money incomes, Muellbauer
(1978) reported that:

> The real gross income growth at the bottom decile mean level
> was 2.69 per cent per annum. At the top decile mean income
> level it was 2.75 per cent per annum. Thus, comparing the
> top of the distribution with the bottom, the modest equalis-
> ing trend in money incomes (of around 0.6 per cent per
> annum) over 1957 to 1974 *is more than wiped out by dif-
> ferential inflation.* (p. 331, our emphasis)

More recent evidence is available from calculations made by
the Low Pay Unit in the construction of a regular monthly price
index for the low paid, published jointly with the CPSA. The
Low Paid Price Index (LPPI) measures the monthly changes in
the average prices of goods and services bought by the lowest
decile of wage earners. A corresponding High Paid Price Index
(HPPI), relating to the highest decile of wage-earners, allows
comparison of the relative impact of inflation on the low and
high paid. The LPPI was first calculated for November 1977 when
it showed that prices facing the low paid had increased by 93.2
per cent since January 1974. The corresponding increase for
the high paid was 89.7 per cent, $3\frac{1}{2}$ percentage points less than
for the low paid. The differential grew wider over the following
14 months and stood at 6.7 percentage points in January 1979.
By the middle of 1979 the gap had closed once again, and for a
brief period in early 1980 the low paid were actually being hit
less hard by inflation than the high paid. Over the following
year, however, the more familiar pattern reasserted itself.
Thanks to exceptionally high increases in the prices of gas
(+ 25 per cent), electricity (+ 23 per cent), tobacco (+ 23 per
cent) domestic rates (+ 21 per cent) and rents (+ 40 per cent)
the LPPI stood at 310.2 in June 1981 (January 1974 = 100), a
full 8.1 percentage points higher than the HPPI. For their
gross real earnings to have stayed the same, relative to one
another, over the period January 1974 to June 1981 the money
earnings of the low paid would have had to have increased by
nearly 8 per cent more than the increase in the salaries of the

high paid. Since the earnings of the highest decile of male
wage-earners increased by 25 per cent *more* than the increase
in earnings enjoyed by the lowest decile between 1974 and 1981,
it is likely that the real wages of the lowest decile have declined
considerably, in relation to those of the highest decile, over the
period.

TAX AVOIDANCE AND EVASION

In our earlier discussion of the official statistics on income
distribution, we drew attention to the vulnerability of essentially
tax-based statistics to under-recording of incomes. We also
noted that this under-recording was likely to be greater for
certain elements of income – income in kind, self-employment
incomes, investment incomes and capital gains – which are of
greater importance to high income groups. This means that,
at any point in time, the distribution of income is likely to be
much less equal than the official figures suggest. And if the
importance of these forms of income is increasing over time,
our assessment of the change in inequality will once again need
to be modified.

The suggestion that the size of unreported incomes was both
large and growing was given by Sir William Pile, Chairman of the
Board of Inland Revenue, in evidence to the House of Commons
Expenditure Committee in March 1979. Sir William told the Committee that it was not implausible that unreported income
amounted to as much as 7½ per cent of GDP, or an annual total
of £10 billion (House of Commons, 1979). He also reported that,
in the Inland Revenue's view, the problem had been growing
over the previous ten years.

Two year's later, Sir William Pile's successor as Chairman of
the Inland Revenue was again asked by the House of Commons
Public Accounts Committee if he could estimate the likely extent
of unrecorded income. Sir Lawrence Airey confirmed that the
figure of 7½ per cent of GDP was still plausible, now representing total unreported income of £16 billion (House of Commons,
1981). This suggested a tax loss of about £4 billion, equivalent
to about 20 per cent of the entire yield from income tax.

The estimate by Sir William Pile had implied that one income-
earner in every eight was not declaring £1,000 of his or her
income every year. Of course, this is an average figure. The
opportunities for avoidance and evasion vary widely according
to the source of income. As the Royal Commission (1979)
reported: 'An employee has much less opportunity for under-
representing his income because this would normally require
the collusion of the person operating the PAYE system and
because the provisions concerning allowable expenses are more
restrictive' (p. 212).

Some light was thrown on the growth and differential extent
of under-reporting by a study carried out by the Central

Statistical Office. By comparing national statistics on income
with equivalent data on expenditure they found that the 'hidden
economy' grew dramatically between 1972 and 1978. Some of
this increase was attributable to a growth in under-reported
wages, salaries and profits, but most was due to a large jump
in unreported incomes from self-employment. In 1978, more
than one-fifth of self-employment incomes (21 per cent) went
unreported compared with 8 per cent in 1972. In the case of
employees, only 0.3 per cent of incomes went unreported in
1972, a figure that had risen to 1 per cent by 1978. In both
years under-reported incomes from self-employment accounted
for over three-quarters of all under-reported incomes (MacAfee,
1980).

As with incomes from self-employment, the opportunities for
under-reporting of fringe benefits are similarly large. We have
noted that the tax liability of such income in kind is negligible.
Employers are required to complete a separate form giving
details of fringe benefits (mainly company cars) for each
employee earning more than £8,500 a year. However, the Inland
Revenue has no information on the numbers of such forms it
distributes each year, the number returned, or the amount of
tax lost because the forms are not completed correctly. When
the Chairman of the Inland Revenue was questioned by the
House of Commons Committee on Public Accounts on the Board's
failure to follow up such infringements he replied 'it is a question of resources ... and this may not necessarily be the highest
priority' (House of Commons, 1981, p. 35).

Under-reporting of income, therefore, has a selective effect
on the official income statistics. Instead of reducing the overall
level by some given factor, the effect on certain forms of
income is disproportionate. While acknowledging that some
forms of under-reported income, such as that from moonlighting
and casual work, may supplement lower incomes, the evidence
does seem to suggest that the greatest effect is at the higher
levels.

In the preceding pages we have singled out three aspects of
inequality which are not fully recorded in the official statistics
– fringe benefits, relative price changes, and tax avoidance and
evasion. In each case, the evidence would lead us to the conclusion that inequality in incomes is somewhat greater than the
official figures suggest and that the change over time in relative income shares may have differed from the official presentation. Differential inflation alone is sufficient to wipe out the
very modest recorded reduction in inequality. If we also take
account of fringe benefits and other forms of unrecorded income,
our conclusion might be that the distribution is somewhat less
equal than it was immediately after the war.

In concluding this section, we should perhaps defer to the
work of Richard Titmuss (1962), who in 1960 set out to examine
the official statistics on income distribution and their assertion
of increased equality. Titmuss concluded:

we know less about the economic and social structure of our society than we thought we did. ... We would be much more hesitant in suggesting that any equalising forces at work in Britain since 1938 can be promoted to the status of 'natural law' and projected into the future ... there are other forces, deeply rooted in the social structure and fed by many complex institutional factors inherent in large-scale economies, operating in reverse directions. Some of the more critical of these factors, closely linked with the distribution of power, and containing within themselves the seeds of long-lasting effects ... function as concealed multipliers of inequality. (p. 198)

Although there have been some improvements in the official statistics on income distribution in the last twenty years, those forms of income which the statistics are poorly equipped to measure have also grown. Titmuss's conclusion may be still more relevant today.

RECENT CHANGES IN INCOME DISTRIBUTION

The data we have been using up to now, the Blue Book tables prepared by the CSO, provide us with a picture (albeit partial) of changes in the distribution of income up until 1978-9. It will be some time before we will be able to make a proper assessment of the effects of the post-1979 Thatcher government, formally committed to an increase in inequality. We may be able to get a glimpse of more recent changes, however, by piecing together information on the main components of income, principally earnings and social security benefits. Although we have some information on the incomes of top earners as well, the jigsaw will remain incomplete for some time to come.

EARNINGS INEQUALITIES

The main source of information on earnings is the annual 'New Earnings Survey' (NES) carried out by the Department of Employment. The NES is a detailed and valuable survey, providing a great deal of information on the distribution, level and composition of earnings as well as differences by hours of work, age, industry, occupation, region and sex. The survey has its drawbacks; it is based on a 1 per cent sample (drawn from national insurance records) but for some groups the representation is much less than 1 per cent. As with the SPI, those whose earnings are below the national insurance exemption limit (£27 a week in 1981-2) are excluded from the sample. A relatively large proportion of the lowest paid part-timers and young workers are missing. Since the returns are completed by employers there is an inevitable tendency for response to be lower, or for the information to be less accurate, amongst smaller and lower paying establishments. This may especially be the case where a firm is covered by minimum wage rates specified by a wages council. Like the SPI and the FES, the NES also suffers from an under-representation of the highest income recipients, and excludes information on fringe benefits.

Table 2.5 shows how the distribution of earnings of both men and women changed during the 1970s.

TABLE 2.5 *Dispersion of gross weekly earnings, 1970-82 (Male full-time workers aged twenty-one and over; female full-time workers aged eighteen and over whose pay was not affected by absence)*

| | As percentage of the corresponding median | | | | |
	Lowest decile	Lower quartile	Upper quartile	Highest decile	Mean
All men					
1970	65.4	79.7	126.7	160.6	110.3
1971	66.1	80.3	126.5	160.7	110.4
1972	65.5	79.7	126.4	160.9	109.9
1973	65.6	79.9	125.3	158.5	109.1
1974	66.8	80.7	124.6	157.0	108.8
1975	67.0	81.0	125.3	157.6	108.6
1976	67.6	81.3	125.6	159.5	109.1
1977	68.1	81.4	125.6	157.7	108.8
1978	66.8	80.6	125.1	157.9	108.6
1979	66.0	80.3	125.1	156.9	108.0
1980	65.9	80.1	126.5	161.6	109.9
1981	65.6	79.8	129.5	167.7	111.1
1982	64.5	79.0	129.8	168.1	111.0
All women					
1970	66.4	79.8	129.3	170.4	111.8
1971	66.6	80.2	127.3	165.8	110.2
1972	65.6	79.6	128.6	167.1	110.4
1973	67.4	80.7	127.6	164.7	110.4
1974	67.7	81.0	126.4	159.1	108.9
1975	67.4	81.5	125.2	164.5	109.6
1976	66.1	80.2	125.9	165.9	109.0
1977	68.6	82.1	124.7	162.1	108.6
1978	69.1	82.2	125.3	161.4	108.8
1979	69.4	82.1	124.7	158.6	107.9
1980	68.4	81.3	126.1	161.3	108.9
1981	68.0	80.6	129.8	172.6	111.0
1982	66.9	79.7	129.4	169.0	110.1

Source: Department of Employment (1982), Table 30.

Over the whole twelve-year period covered by the table, there was relatively little change in the distribution of earnings. Between 1974 and 1977 there appears to have been a slight improve-

ment in the relative earnings of the lowest decile of both men
and women. This may be partly explained by the effects of the
first three stages of the Wilson government's pay policy, which
nominally favoured the low paid (through flat-rate limits and
minimum wage targets). The effect, however, was small. In
1974, the lowest decile of men earned 66.8 per cent of the
median wage; by 1977 this had increased to 68.1 per cent.
After 1977, the relative earnings of the low paid deteriorated
once more. In the case of low paid women workers, there was a
continuing slight increase even after 1977, perhaps as a result
of the effects of the Equal Pay Act. But since 1979 they have
also suffered a decline in their position.

The period 1977-9 also witnessed some decrease in the relative earnings of the highest decile of men but this was more
than made up for between 1979 and 1981 when the highest
decile increased from 156.9 to 167.7 per cent of the median.
The highest decile of female earnings followed a similarly
dramatic path, jumping from 158.6 per cent of its median in
1979 to 172.6 in 1981, before falling back slightly to 169.0 in
1982.

Between 1979 and 1981 it appears that the gap between manual
and non-manual male workers widened considerably. The earnings of the average male manual worker increased by just 31
per cent (£29 a week), while the average male white-collar
worker received a 44 per cent pay rise over the year and the
best paid tenth of white-collar men enjoyed an increase of over
47 per cent (£80 per week). These figures exclude any additional increases due to annual increments, bonus payments,
promotions or fringe benefits. They therefore understate the
widening of the gap between blue- and white-collar workers.
A similar picture emerges for women's pay. On average, non-
manual women workers enjoyed pay rises of 47 per cent over
the year. Manual women workers got only 35 per cent. Again,
the already better paid received larger percentage increases.

Part of the reason for this widening gap is that the recession
is hitting poorer manual workers harder than better paid non-
manual employees, particularly through cutbacks in overtime.
Only 47 per cent of manual men worked overtime in 1981, compared with 59 per cent in 1974. Yet in 1981 almost a sixth of
manual men still worked more than 10 hours overtime a week,
compared with only 3 per cent of white-collar men. More than
600,000 male manual workers in 1980 escaped low pay only by
working overtime. One effect of the recession will be to push
more of the low paid and their families into poverty.

Looking at pay inequalities overall, the Department of Employment (1981) concludes, 'generally the distribution of earnings,
having narrowed between 1970 and 1979 has widened slightly in the
past two years'. This is clearly true from the official figures:
the top tenth of non-manual men received 3.2 times the earnings
of the poorest tenth of manual men in 1981, compared with only
2.8 times in 1979. But the DoE adds, 'it should be remembered,

however, that these distributions reflect earnings before tax,
the principal instrument of income redistribution' (Department
of Employment, 1981). Quite so. The tax burden of the poorest
workers actually increased between 1979 and 1981, whereas the
best paid enjoyed very substantial income tax cuts.

What is true over the past year or eighteen months has also
been true for a longer period. Looking back to 1975 we find that
the average male manual worker earned 86 per cent of the wage
of his white-collar counterpart. By 1981, his relative wage had
fallen to 77 per cent (Pond, 1981).

The information given above related to the structure of earnings, but not to the changes in the earnings of particular
individuals. Department of Employment analyses of individuals'
earnings have shown that people can move about freely within
the earnings distribution without the shape of the overall distribution changing. As some receive very large increases, lifting
them out of the lowest ranges, somebody else takes their place,
either by undergoing a cut in wages or entering the job market
for the first time (Department of Employment, 1977). Looking
at the period 1970-4, the Department found that cash increases
for manual men ranged between £9.80 and £18.30, while non-
manual men received cash increases of between £17.80 and
£39.40 over that same period. For all non-manual men, percentage increases over that period represented an average of 65.2
per cent, compared with 61.8 per cent for manual men. So if
we look at the earnings of individuals, rather than of 'jobs'
reflected in the whole distribution, the picture of reduced
differentials changes fundamentally.

An analysis of the NES data shows how individuals' earnings
have changed during each financial year from 1973 to 1980. In
four years out of seven non-manual workers achieved bigger
increases in average earnings than manual workers. The situation was reversed in only two years - 1974-5 and 1978-9 - and
in the remaining year the average increase was the same for
both groups. There were few occupational groups in which
individuals consistently increased their earnings by more than
the average increase. Only three groups (professional and
related supporting management and administration; professional
and related in science, engineering, technology and similar
fields; and security and protective services) achieved above
average increases in earnings in five or more years out of
seven. Of the six groups whose earnings increased by less than
the average in five or more years out of seven, all but one
were manual. Between April 1979 and April 1980 all except one
of the non-manual occupations enjoyed above average increases
in earnings while only two out of nine non-manual groups
managed to do likewise.

The effect that these movements in wages and salaries have
had on occupational differentials over the past six years can
be seen from the NES data which suggest that most of the
occupational groups earning less than the average in 1974 had

experienced a worsening of their position by 1980. Only three
groups – security and protective service; selling; and catering,
cleaning, etc. – managed to move their average earnings closer
to the national average between 1979 and 1980. And only four
groups were closer to the national average in 1980 than they
had been in 1974.

At the other end of the scale there is some evidence of a
reduction in differentials between 1974 and 1979. All groups
with above average earnings in 1974 had moved closer to the
average by 1979. In the following year, however, the differentials widened once again, although professionals and
related in education, welfare and health did not enjoy as big
an improvement as their counterparts in management and administration or those in science, engineering and technology.

As we noted above, the NES data do not adequately cover the
highest earning occupational groups – company directors and
supporting top management. We can get some idea of the movement in their salaries, however, from the annual salary surveys
carried out by the British Institute of Management (BIM). From
these surveys it appears that the 'captains of industry' have
suffered something of a relative decline in their gross earnings;
but it was not as dramatic a decline as might have been expected.
Worst affected have been the chief executives, whose average
gross salaries have fallen from 637 per cent of the national
average male wage in 1974, to 489 per cent in 1981, and deputy
chief executives, whose salaries have fallen from 543 per cent
to 453 per cent of the national average. Other top management
salaries have suffered a less dramatic decline, concentrated
largely between 1974 and 1977. Since 1977 their salaries stayed
about the same or improved slightly.

TABLE 2.6 *Directors' average gross earnings as a percentage of average gross
male earnings, 1974-81*

	1974	1975	1976	1977	1978	1979	1980	1981
Chief executive	637	569	553	541	565	557	527	489
Deputy chief executive	543	500	541	460	507	487	481	453
Other directors	437	407	408	374	381	383	368	362
Senior heads of function	316	295	302	274	289	291	293	291
Other heads of function	272	256	251	232	247	249	258	239

Source: British Institute of Management (1977, 1981).

Piecing together the data that we have presented regarding
recent movement in the distribution of earned incomes, it would
seem that there may have been some movement towards greater
equality during the mid-1970s with some restoration of the
dispersion after 1977. We need to be careful, however, in interpreting the results. The data available relate only to the

average earnings of different groups. As we noted above,
the experience of individuals within those groups may be very
different. As Guy Routh (1980) has pointed out, the dispersion
of pay within occupations can be as great, if not greater, as
that between occupations. The distinction between the earnings
of groups and those of individuals is particularly important in
the case of professionals and managers, who are normally subject to pay structures with a steep incline, and who normally
receive annual increments. If a senior manager retires and
is replaced by a younger successor on a lower salary this will
tend to depress the recorded increase in the earnings of
managers as a whole, while the experience of the individuals
is much more favourable. And we should remember that the
salary figures presented here are before the inclusion of fringe
benefits, which increased dramatically from the mid-1970s
onwards.

WELFARE BENEFITS

No picture of the distribution of income would be complete without some consideration of the value of cash welfare benefits,
which now represent the major – and in many cases the only –
source of income for a growing proportion of the population.
While the scope and value of fringe benefits grew apace throughout the 1970s, the same was not true of national insurance and
social security benefits. The early years of the 1974-9 Labour
government's term of office did witness some improvement in the
relative value of such benefits. But since 1976 their value has
declined or, at best, stagnated.
    Over a period when registered unemployment rose from 1.4
million (November 1976) to 2.2 million (November 1980) it is the
unemployed who have suffered the biggest loss in income. Having increased from 38.7 per cent of net average earnings in
1973 to 44.1 per cent in 1976, by 1980 the standard rate of
unemployment benefit for a married couple had fallen back to
39.4 per cent. The single person's benefit similarly fell over
the same period from 28.7 per cent of net average earnings to
25.7 per cent. Those dependent on welfare benefits should not
be too excited by the fact that our estimates suggest that the
value of benefits will rise slightly, relative to net average
earnings, in November 1981. This apparent improvement is, in
fact, a result of the government's decision to raise National
Insurance contributions by 1 per cent (as of April 1981) and
its failure to increase personal tax allowances in line with inflation. Both of these decisions have helped to pull average net
earnings down nearer to welfare benefit levels, bringing an
illusionary 'improvement' in the position of benefit claimants.
    The relative value of child support has also fallen in recent
years. After falling steadily throughout the 1950s and 1960s,
the value of family allowances/child benefits and child tax

allowances staged something of a recovery between 1975 and 1979, over which period support for a single child family rose from 3 per cent of average earnings to 4.5 per cent. Since 1979, however, the value of child benefit has been allowed to fall back once again, reaching an estimated 3.7 per cent of average earnings in April 1981.

TABLE 2.7 *The changing value of cash welfare benefits*

	As a percentage of male net average earnings				
	1973	1976	1979	1980	1981[b]
Standard rate for single person					
Unemployment Benefit	24.8	28.7	26.4	25.7	26.4
Supplementary Benefit[a]	27.5	34.8	33.9	33.8	34.7
Retirement Pension	26.1	34.0	33.3	33.8	34.7
Standard rate for married couple:					
Unemployment Benefit	38.7	44.1	40.6	39.4	40.6
Supplementary Benefit[a]	41.8	52.3	51.0	51.2	52.8
Retirement Pension	40.7	51.7	50.6	51.2	52.8

Notes: a. Long-term scale rates. b. Estimated using National Institute of Economic and Social Research forecast of 8.4 per cent wage inflation, November 1980-November 1981.
Source: 'Hansard', 3 March 1981, cols 85-6.

The information available on changes in the distribution of incomes since 1978-9 is inevitably partial and incomplete. The evidence available at the time of writing suggests that the recession, combined with the effects of government policies, have tended to widen economic inequalities in the most recent past. The effects have been selective: the deepening of the recession, by increasing unemployment, reducing hours of work and depressing wage rises has had a differentially harsh effect on those most vulnerable in the labour market. Reductions in state expenditure after 1977 have also affected most those at the lower end of the income distribution. And, as Frank Field shows in the following chapter, tax changes have been working in the same direction. When the official figures on income distribution of the late 1970s and early 1980s become available they will no doubt demonstrate that Mrs Thatcher's government has effectively conferred, on rich and poor alike, 'the right to be unequal'.

Breaking the mould:
the Thatcher government's
fiscal policies

Frank Field

This chapter looks at the fiscal measures taken by the Thatcher
government in its attempt to change the distribution of income
and wealth. The first section gives a brief summary of the
distribution of income and wealth and the changing burden of
taxation in the period before Mrs Thatcher's 1979 election win.
The second section outlines the main fiscal changes on income
and capital since 1979 and the final section calculates the
distributional impact of these changes.

Using the official data on the distribution of pre-taxed income,
we find the following changes in the post-war period. The income
share going to the richest 1 per cent of the population has
been halved since 1949 and stood at 5.5 per cent in 1977-8. And
while the richest 2 to 5 per cent of the population has seen a
much smaller decline in its pre-taxed income, the richest 6 to
10 per cent slightly improved its position. Overall, the income
of the country's richest 10 per cent declined from around a
third of all incomes in 1949 to a quarter in 1977-8. Yet this
decline did not result in any significant redistribution to those
at the bottom half of the income distribution. In 1949-50 the
least well off 50 per cent of the population gained 23.7 per cent
of pre-taxed income and by 1976-7 their pre-taxed income was
still less than 25 per cent. The redistribution from the top 10
per cent found its way into the pockets of those in the next
four deciles in the earnings league whose share of pre-taxed
income rose by 6 percentage points.

The post-tax distribution of income shows smaller changes
than that which occurred in the pre-taxed distribution. The
richest 1 per cent's share of income fell in the period since
1949 from $5\frac{1}{2}$ per cent to just under 4 per cent. The share of
the richest 10 per cent was reduced from 26 per cent to 23 per
cent and the share of the poorest 10 per cent rose from 2.5 per
cent to 3 per cent.

What have been the major changes in the distribution of wealth? While the Royal Commission estimated that during the last three decades the wealth-holdings of the rich were reduced by 0.7 per cent a year, Atkinson and Harrison estimated that over a much larger time-span - from 1923 to 1972 - the annual reduction has been nearer 0.4 per cent. As Chris Pond comments in his chapter, at this pace of redistribution, the top 1 per cent will still be in possession of one-fifth of all personal wealth by the end of the century. Currently, the richest 1 per cent's holding in wealth is as great as that possessed by the bottom 50 per cent of the population, and while the average wealth-holding of the poorest 50 per cent of the population is less than £1,000, the average wealth stake of the richest 1 per cent is around a quarter of a million pounds.

TAX BURDEN UP TO 1979

How is it that the tax burden has risen significantly in the post-war period and yet inequalities in the distribution of income and wealth are still so very marked? To begin answering this question we need to examine how the incidence of taxation has affected different income groups during the post-war period, and this information will provide an important backcloth for a review of the changes in the tax burden since 1979.

Two trends are discernible in the changing burden of direct taxation in the period up to the advent of the Thatcher government and both can be seen from an examination of what is called the tax threshold - the point at which a person's income becomes taxable. An examination of the threshold for different tax-paying units - single person, married couple, married couple with different numbers of children - shows the following changes. In 1949-50, while the single person began to pay tax at a fraction below 40 per cent of average earnings, a married couple with one wage packet did not contribute a penny in direct taxation until they earned almost 63 per cent of average earnings. In the last tax year before Mrs Thatcher's win at the polls the tax threshold for a single person and married couple had fallen respectively to 21.8 per cent and 34 per cent of average earnings. A married couple with two children with only one wage earner began paying income tax at a fraction below average earnings in 1949-50 and this group's tax threshold had fallen to 42.6 per cent of average earnings by 1978-9. A family with four children was exempt in 1949-50 from tax until their income was more than 130 per cent of average earnings. At the end of the Callaghan government their tax threshold had fallen to less than 52 per cent of average earnings.

So while it is true to say that the tax threshold fell for all types of income taxpayers before Mrs Thatcher's 1979 election win, it did not fall equally fast for all groups. Over the period

from 1949-50 to 1978-9 the tax threshold fell by 45 per cent for
a single person and by 46 per cent for a married couple. Much
more significant reductions were recorded for households with
children. For a married couple with one child under 11 the tax
threshold fell by 54 per cent. For a married couple with two
children the fall was 57 per cent. The larger the family the
more significant was the fall in the tax threshold measured as a
percentage of average earnings. A family with three children
saw a reduction in the tax threshold of 59 per cent and for a
four-child family the reduction was 60 per cent.

These changes in the tax thresholds show the two important
shifts in the tax burden in the period up to 1979. Over the
years more and more people on lower and lower incomes have
been called upon to pay direct tax and consequently the number
of tax-paying units jumped from 13.5 million in 1945 to 21.3
million in 1978-9. But this vertical shift in the burden of taxation has not been shared equally; the burden of tax has
increased fastest for taxpayers responsible for children. This
is what is meant when we talk about the horizontal shift in the
incidence of taxation and it is important to look at the combined
effect of both the vertical and horizontal shift in the tax burden
for the years up to 1979.

It is those on average and below average earnings who have
seen the greatest percentage increase in the proportion of their
income taken in tax and national insurance deductions. Starting
the analysis in 1949-50 and continuing up to 1978-9 the share of
contributions to the Exchequer for a single person on two-thirds
average earnings increased 119 per cent. For a married couple
the increase was in the order of 251 per cent, falling to 240
per cent for a married couple with two children and 193 per
cent for a married couple with four children.

The pattern is somewhat different for those on average
earnings. For a single person the tax contributions increased
by 92 per cent. For a married couple the increase recorded
was 160 per cent but a married couple with two children on
average earnings saw a 606 per cent increase in their tax
contributions in the period up to 1979 and a couple with four
children experienced a similar increase - a rise of 556 per cent.

Taxpayers with children, whatever their level of earnings,
experienced a faster increase in their tax burden compared with
single taxpayers on the same level of earnings. A single person
on twice average earnings, for example, experienced a 35 per
cent rise in his tax bill, while a family with four children on the
same level of earnings saw their contribution to the Exchequer
rise by 231 per cent in the years up to 1979. And yet the higher
the income of taxpayers the smaller the difference in the percentage increase in the proportion of earnings paid in tax and
national insurance between those who are single taxpayers and
those with children. The reason for this is that as we move into
the higher income brackets the income base becomes large
enough to begin to disguise the extra burden of tax which has

been placed on households with children. A single person earning five times average earnings saw their tax bill rise by 61 per cent whereas a household with four children on the same level of income experienced a 91 per cent increase in their contribution to the Exchequer. On ten times average earnings the difference is even less marked; a 50 per cent increase for a single person and a 57 per cent increase for taxpayers with children.

These then are the main changes in the direct tax burden in the period up to 1979 with the greatest increase in contribution coming from those taxpayers on lower income and those with children. In the 1979 general election Mrs Thatcher was elected on a programme of cutting taxation for all groups. How did these two groups, which experienced the largest increase in taxation in recent years, fare from the fiscal changes brought about by Mrs Thatcher's 1979, 1980 and 1981 budgets?

THE BUDGETS

The 1979 budget brought about six major changes in the direct system of taxation: personal allowances were increased by over 18 per cent compared to the previous year; the basic rate of income tax was cut by 3p to 30 per cent; the starting point at which the higher rates of tax become payable was raised from £8,000 to £10,000 of taxable income; the thresholds for the higher rate bands were increased; and the top rate of income tax was reduced from 83 per cent to 60 per cent. At the same time the budget increased the threshold for investment income surcharge to £5,000 for all taxpayers, doubling the threshold for those aged 65 and over and more than doubling it for those under 65. The 10 per cent rate of surcharge was abolished. The 1979 budget also increased the age allowance income limit from £4,000 to £5,000.

The same budget ushered in important changes in indirect taxation in order to help pay for the cuts in direct taxation. Prior to the budget there had been two rates of Value Added Tax for those goods and services which were not zero rated. The budget brought about a unification of the standard and higher rates of tax (8 per cent and 12.5 per cent) into a single 15 per cent rate. Increases were also announced in petrol and DERV duties.

Five major changes in the direct system of taxation were brought about by the 1980 budget. Personal allowances were again increased by around 18 per cent on the previous tax year's level. But to help to pay for this change and, as we will see in the next section, to claw back much of the gain, the Chancellor announced the abolition of the lower rate of tax which was previously levied at 25 per cent on the first £750 of taxable income. The budget increased again the threshold for the higher rates of tax, raising it from £10,000 to £11,250 of

taxable income while at the same time widening some of the
higher rate bands. The threshold for investment income surcharge was raised by £500 to £550 and the age allowance by
£900 to £5,900.

In this, the Thatcher administration's second budget, the
Chancellor again made increases in indirect taxation but on
nothing like the same scale as the previous year. Extra duty
became payable on beer, spirits and tobacco. Likewise, petrol,
DERV and heavy oil duty was increased while the Vehicle Excise
Duty (VED) on cars was raised by £10 a year and on heavy
lorries by around 30 per cent.

In the 1981 budget the Chancellor brought about major changes
in the incidence of taxation by not making any direct tax
changes. Most importantly of all, he announced that the threshold for personal allowances would not be increased in line with
inflation. Since the Lawson/Rooker/Wise Amendment to the
1977 Finance Bill, chancellors have been compelled to increase
the tax threshold by means of increasing the personal allowances
in line with inflation unless they seek the approval of the
House of Commons not to do so. Such approval was sought and
given in the 1981 Finance Act. Changes were, however,
announced in indirect taxes and VED and the duties on alcoholic
drinks, tobacco and road fuel increased.

While National Insurance contributions are levied separately
from income tax, most workers regard these contributions as
part of the system of direct taxation – as indeed they are.
Since 1979 there have also been important changes in the
National Insurance contributions, and particularly those for
employees.

Today the contributions are based on a percentage principle
and the collection of the tax is governed by what is called
a lower and upper earnings limit. In the last year of Labour
government the standard worker's contribution was 6.5 per
cent, the lower earnings limit stood at £17.50 and the upper
earnings limit £120 a week. Workers with earnings below £17.50
a week paid no National Insurance contributions, but a worker
whose income crossed this threshold found that the whole of
his earnings became subject to the 6.5 per cent national insurance levy. At the other end of the earnings scale contributions
ceased on earnings above £120 a week.

Changes in the National Insurance contributions were announced by the Labour government and were brought into force in
April 1979. The standard contribution of 6.5 per cent was maintained, but the earnings limits were adjusted, being raised to
£19.50 a week for the lower level and the upper level or ceiling,
as it is usually called, raised to £135. In the following year the
government increased the standard worker's contribution by
0.25 per cent, raising it to 6.75 per cent. Likewise, changes
were made to the lower and upper earnings limit, the new figures
being £23 and £165 a week respectively. Even bigger increases
were brought into effect in April 1981 with the standard

worker's contribution rising a whole percentage point to 7.75 per cent and the lower and upper earnings limit increased to £27 and £200 a week, and a further one percentage point increase (to 8.75 per cent) on weekly earnings between £29.50 and £220 has been announced to take effect from April 1982.

A third range of fiscal changes has been brought about by the Thatcher government relating to the taxation of capital. In his chapter Chris Pond details the fall in revenue from capital taxes and yet, in his 1979 budget, the Chancellor stated his determination to make the taxation of capital not only 'simpler' but 'less oppressive'. Sir Geoffrey Howe referred to the Capital Gains Tax (CGT) as 'a capricious and sometimes savage levy on capital itself'. Likewise he viewed the Capital Transfer Tax (CTT) as 'harmful to business, and a real deterrent to initiative and enterprise' but because the issues involved in both these taxes were 'difficult and complex' the Chancellor left any reforms until his budget in March 1980 when he made changes to the operation of the Capital Transfer Tax and the Capital Gains Tax.

In his second 1980 budget the Chancellor doubled the threshold for CTT to £50,000. Threshold changes were also made to CGT. Previously, on gains over £5,000, a £1,000 exemption on the capital gain had been progressively withdrawn. This system was disbanded and the Chancellor announced that a new £3,000 exemption would be introduced. In the following year, March 1981, further changes were made in the capital transfer tax. A major restructuring occurred which converted the tax into a short-term capital levy in all but name. A rich couple can give away £160,000 tax free every ten years (or, as Alister Sutherland shows, £320,000 tax free every decade if the assets enjoy the 50 per cent valuation reduction for business or farmers' assets). In addition, the annual exemption for capital transferred was raised to £3,000. Additional changes were made to the taxation of let agricultural land. Agricultural land has a 50 per cent exemption from any CTT, and the 1981 budget instituted a 20 per cent exemption on the capital levy for all agricultural land which was left. The interest-free instalments for repayments were extended to any levy charged on let agricultural land and the limit of £250,000 on the repayment was also removed.

WHO GOT WHAT?

The cuts in income tax in the 1979 budget were probably the largest single reduction in the burden of direct taxation (measured as a percentage of GDP) ever brought about by any Chancellor of the Exchequer. We have already described the form these tax cuts took but who gained most from them? A distributional analysis shows that the tax cuts were directed overwhelmingly at higher income groups and taxpayers without

children. From the 1979 budget changes the poorest 10 per cent
of taxpayers, for example, gained only 2 per cent of the £4.6
billion reduction in taxation. In contrast, the richest 1 per
cent of taxpayers cornered 15 per cent of the total tax cuts and
the top 7 per cent of taxpayers (those earning in excess of
£10,000 in 1979-80) gained between them £1.6 billion, or 34 per
cent of the tax handouts.

It is also possible to examine the gains from the 1979 budget
for individual taxpayers on different levels of income. Taxpayers earning less than £2,000 a year saw a £45 reduction in
their tax bill. For those earning between £2,000 and £4,000
the average gain per tax unit amounted to £95. In contrast,
taxpayers earning above £20,000 a year gained an average of
£3,850 per tax unit, and these tax cuts remain in force until
they are evoked by a future budget. The richest 7 per cent
of taxpayers have therefore benefited to a tune of £4.8 billion
in the three years following the 1979 budget, and this takes
into account only the 1979 tax changes (Field, 1979a).

As well as this vertical redistribution the 1979 budget brought
about a further horizontal redistribution, this time from taxpayers with children to childless taxpayers. Up until the abolition of child tax allowance the taxpaying capacity of families
with children was taken account of (although admittedly less
than adequately) by adjustment to child tax allowances (CTAs).
Since 1979 (with the abolition of CTAs) chancellors have to
increase child benefit if they wish to maintain equity in the
tax free income of households with children compared with
childless taxpayers. In his 1979 budget Sir Geoffrey Howe
announced only a small change in the additional child benefit
paid to single parents. This uprating cost £8 million, at a time
when the total tax cuts amounted to £4.6 billion. And although
subsequent increases in child benefit have been made - a 75p
increase in November 1980 and a further 50p rise a year later -
its real value has fallen with a result that the tax burden of
families at the start of 1982 had increased faster than for other
groups of taxpayers.

The 1980 budget increased personal allowances in line with
inflation, but part of this increase (6.8 per cent) was effectively
clawed back by the abolition of the reduced band of tax. The
higher rate threshold was also increased and the overall effect
of the three moves was once again to decrease most the tax
burden of higher income groups. The abolition of the 25 per
cent tax on the first £750 of taxable income increased every
taxpayer's tax by 72p a week, no matter how small or large was
their income. In contrast, the personal allowance changes
resulted in tax reductions of only 55p a week for a taxpayer
with a £40 wage packet, £1.15 on a £100 wage packet and £3.46
on a £250 a week wage packet. However, some taxpayers also
gained an additional tax reduction as a result of the indexation
of the higher rate threshold, and this sum became larger the
higher the taxpayer's weekly income, amounting, for example,

to a £10.09 reduction on earnings of £600 a week.

The overall effect of the 1980 budget was similar to that of the previous year, with the richest taxpayers cornering the lion's share of the tax reductions. The cost of the 1980 tax changes was in the region of £1.5 billion and of this sum the richest 2 per cent of taxpayers gained around one seventh of the total – almost £200 million.

The main characteristic of the 1981 budget was the failure to index personal allowances. Speaking in the 1980 budget, the Chancellor was clear on the consequences of his vetoing the indexation measure. He recalled that such an action:

> would lower the starting point of income tax in real terms, compared with a year ago. It would increase the numbers of taxpayers. It would narrow the gap between the tax threshold and the main social security benefits, and would impose particularly heavy burdens on those with the smallest incomes. All these effects would be most undesirable. ('Hansard', 26 March 1980, col. 1474)

Failure to raise the tax threshold in line with inflation had the very effects of which the Chancellor forewarned a year earlier. Had thresholds been fully indexed in the 1981 budget the single persons' and married couples' allowances for 1981-2 would have been increased to £1,585 and £2,475 respectively. Non-indexation resulted in a cut in the tax threshold equivalent to £4.04 a week for a single person and £6.35 for a married couple. As a result, and in the government's own calculations, an additional million and a quarter more people were brought into the tax net.

The government's defence was that it needed to raise additional funds and its failure to honour the indexing commitment resulted in a revenue bonus of £2.5 billion. A subsidiary defence was, in the words of the Chancellor, that: 'it does enable us to avoid, and I am sure it is right, the need for any change in the basic rates of tax'. But for whom is it right?

To raise the same amount of revenue would have required a 3p increase in the basic tax rate and this change has a different distributional impact to what amounted to a 15 per cent cut in the real value of personal allowances. Any family earning less than £109 a week would have found themselves better off had the Chancellor raised the additional revenue by increasing the rate of tax rather than cutting the value of personal allowances. The difference for a family on £75 a week is a little over £1. Taxpayers on £200 a week lost £1.85 by the government's failure to increase personal allowances but would have faced an increased weekly tax bill of £4.58 from a 3p increase in the standard rate of tax, and this difference becomes more marked the higher one moves up the income scale.

EFFECT ON THE POOR

In each of the three budgets the Chancellor enacted measures which were of most advantage to higher taxpayers. Tax and National Insurance contributions for taxpayers on five and ten times average earnings, for example, have been reduced from 50.5 per cent and 60.5 per cent of gross earnings to 43.2 per cent and 51.6 per cent respectively by 1982. But at the same time these gains to the very rich were paid for disproportionately by poorer taxpayers. The tax load for earners on two-thirds average earnings has risen from 21.9 per cent to 24 per cent of gross earnings by 1982. The dangers to this group were clearly in the Chancellor's mind when, in his 1979 budget, he observed that:

> it is not only at the top end of the income range that the burden of income tax is particularly oppressive, the same is true for those on the lowest taxable incomes, where the tax system can help to ensure that some people are actually better off out of work. That is the importance of the tax thresholds. ('Hansard', 12 June 1979, col. 259)

The decision not to index the personal allowances in the 1981 budget, the abolition of the reduced band of tax in 1980 and the failure during the years since 1979 to maintain the real value of child benefits, have all played a key part in deepening and a widening of the poverty trap and exacerbating the 'why work?' syndrome.

The phrase 'poverty trap' was coined to describe those income bands over which the net income of low paid workers increases little, if at all. The 'why work?' syndrome is the phrase used by Ralph Howell to highlight the lack of incentives for those out of work whose only prospect when jobs are available is of low paid employment. Table 3.1 gives the key information on the tax threshold and eligibility for the Family Income Supplement which is important when looking at the poverty trap. It also includes the supplementary benefit income levels which are crucial in any consideration of the 'why work?' syndrome.

The poverty trap is the nightmare in which may low wage earning families with children find themselves. As soon as his income passes beyond the tax threshold, the low wage earner not only has a tax reduction of 30p in the pound but to this sum is added the National Insurance contribution (8.75p from April 1982) on all income once his earnings rise above £29.50. Moreover, as the low-wage-earner's income rises, his eligibility for other means-tested benefits comes under review, although the review rarely takes place at the same time as the person gains a wage increase. For each increased one pound in earnings, his eligibility for FIS is reduced by 50p when his benefit is next computed. Similarly, for each one pound increase in earnings, a person begins to lose eligibility for rent and rate

TABLE 3.1 *Tax thresholds and poverty line incomes 1979-81 for a two-child family[a] (£p per week)*

	tax threshold[d]	SB income[c]	FIS level
1979[b]	34.90	48.70	60.50
1980	41.25	58.00	74.00
1981	41.25	65.45	82.00

Notes: a. aged under 10 years. b. tax thresholds effective from April and social security rates for the November of each year. c. assuming rent levels of £6.50 in 1979, £8.80 in 1980 and £11.90 in 1981. d. married person's allowance, wife assumed not to be working.
Source: Social Security Statistics 1981, Tables 34.01 and 32.01.

rebates. The income bands over which the poverty trap has operated since 1979 can be seen in Table 3.2 which shows that the trap now operates over a wider band of income in 1981 than when the government took office in 1979. The Low Pay Unit has calculated an increase of almost 40 per cent in the numbers of families caught in the poverty trap – up from 80,000 to 110,000 – since the government took office.

TABLE 3.2 *Poverty trap income bands 1979-81*

	£/week
November 1979	35 – 60
November 1980	41 – 73
November 1981	42 – 81

Table 3.1 also helps to illustrate the incentives problem for low wage earners which is now often referred to as the 'why work' syndrome. Much of this debate has emphasised how an unemployed low wage earner can find himself worse off when he is able to find work. However, a detailed look at the figures shows that very few unemployed families are made worse off once they are back in work. What is true is that they are financially very little better off once a job has been found.

If we take a two-child unemployed family in 1980, their weekly supplementary benefit entitlement, assuming average rent payments, together with help from other benefits such as free school meals and milk, comes to £66.40. Their rebated rent and rates amounts to £12.35, and so the family's net weekly spending power is £54.05. Let us now assume that the head of this family is offered a job at £30.00 a week. This wage, together with FIS, child benefit and other welfare benefits, brings the total weekly income up to £73.79. From this the low wage earner will have to pay £2.03 in National Insurance contributions,

meet a rebated rent and rates bill of £12.35 and work expenses
of, say, £3.55. This total of £17.93 work of deductions gives a
net weekly spending power of £55.86 – larger than that which
the same family would gain unemployed, but only just.

The benefit which can make a major difference to the net
spending power of low wage working families is child benefit.
Child benefit is tax free and is kept in full by families in work
while being deducted from the benefit income of unemployed
families. The larger the child benefit therefore the larger
becomes the difference in a family's income from work and their
income from benefits.

The poverty lobby has probably been wrong in not stressing
just how minimal are incentives for low wage earners, particularly when comparing their income in and out of work. It was
this aspect, after all, which finally won over the Treasury to
support the introduction of family allowances back in the war
years. And to the extent that the Thatcher government has
failed to maintain the real value of child benefits, and its failure
to index tax thresholds in the 1981 budget, the incentives, or
more accurately the disincentives faced by unemployed low wage
earners seeking work, have become even more acute.

A further cause of the increasing severity of the poverty trap
and the exacerbation of the 'why work?' syndrome has been
the increase in National Insurance contributions since 1979
– largely, though not entirely, due to the need to finance the
ever growing unemployment benefit bill. As we have seen, the
standard contributions rose from 6.5 per cent in 1979 to 7.75
per cent in 1981-2 with a further rise to 8.75 per cent from
April 1982. However, 'the ceiling' on contributions resulted in
taxpayers on twice average earnings having their contributions
raised from 4.5 to 6 per cent of their income and those on five
and ten times average earnings having their contribution raised
from 1.8 per cent and 0.09 per cent to 2.4 and 1.2 per cent
respectively. In money terms this has meant that in 1981-2 a
worker on two-thirds average earnings paid £6.69 in National
Insurance contributions while a worker on ten times average
earnings contributed only £15.50 a week.

INDIRECT TAX CHANGES

Increases in National Insurance contributions have not been the
only fiscal change brought about by the government to increase
its revenue which has weighed most excessively on low income
taxpayers. As we saw earlier, the budgets since 1979 have
brought about a major change in the incidence of direct taxation
in favour of higher income groups, and largely in order to pay
for these tax cuts the government has had to increase the level
of indirect taxation. Most observers believe that indirect taxation is regressive – hitting hardest those on low incomes,
although it is possible to argue, as some government spokesmen

have done, that the major indirect tax, VAT, is not regressive.
The Chancellor used just this argument when presenting his
1979 budget. After reminding the House that large areas of
consumer spending are not chargeable to VAT, Sir Geoffrey
Howe went on to argue that as poorer households spend disproportionately more of their income on zero rated goods 'VAT
is not regressive'. However, to argue in this manner it is
necessary to calculate the effects of VAT on expenditure rather
than on disposable income. Once a person's disposable income
is taken as the base line the regressiveness of indirect tax
becomes more apparent. In 1979 only 2.5 per cent of the top 10
per cent's income, for example, went in VAT. This contrasts
with 3.3 and 3.1 per cent of the incomes of the ninth and tenth
decile respectively.
The view that indirect tax is regressive was the main thrust
of a confidential Minute prepared by the DHSS before the 1979
budget and which later came into the hands of the 'New Statesman'. According to the 'New Statesmen', the Minute stated: 'it
is clear that a shift from income tax to commodity taxation would
help the rich and hurt the poor'. The Minute went on to explain
the distributional impact on the poor of increasing the percentage of total government revenue coming from direct taxation.

the poorest 10 per cent of households pay, at present, considerably more tax on their expenditure than on their income
and this is true even if subsidies are taken into account. This
occurs even though on average the commodity tax payment
by households is lower than the income tax payment and
occurs because the income tax system through its allocation
of tax-free allowances prevents the very poorest from paying tax. In contrast, the income tax payment of the richest
20 per cent of households is nearly double their commodity
tax payment .... over 10 per cent of the commodity tax
burden before subsidies is borne by the poorest 20 per
cent of households compared with only 3.8 per cent of the
income tax burden and 4.7 per cent of National Insurance
contributions.

The Minute went on to argue:

An additional £1 in tax has a greater effect on a pensioner
earning only £30 a week than it does on a millionaire. So to
measure the progressivity or otherwise of a system of taxation it is useful to compare the tax of each household with
its disposable income. The tax could be said to be progressive if the proportion of the disposable income of the poorer
household which is paid in tax is lower than that of richer
households. On this measure, commodity taxation as it
existed in 1977 was regressive. (reproduced in Field, 1981,
p. 104)

The 'New Statesman' emphasised that the poorest 10 per cent paid 19 per cent of their disposable income in commodity tax while the richest 20 per cent paid only 15 per cent. But it is important to remember that these calculations have been made after adding back the effect of rent and rate rebates. Even so, indirect taxation was shown to be regressive even before the 1979 changes which abolished the standard and luxury rates of tax of 8 and 12.5 per cent respectively and instituted a standard 15 per cent VAT rate.

CONCLUSION

The years since 1979 have become a key period in Britain's post-war history. Up to that time it was generally assumed that the effect of the imposition of taxes and the payment of benefits was to lay the basis for an increasingly equal society. This chapter has reviewed the data on the distribution of income and wealth and shown that what equalising forces there have been had far less effect than is commonly assumed. The tax burden certainly increased, but the most marked increases were for those on low income and taxpayers with children.

It is against this background that the tax changes described since 1979 must be judged. The 1979 budget, and to a lesser extent the 1980 budget, brought about a major reduction in the burden of taxation, but not for the low paid or those with children. Overwhelmingly the major gains went to higher income groups and were distributed without any regard to the family responsibilities of taxpayers. Those on average earnings have seen a real reduction in their take-home pay whereas those on five and ten times average earnings are still £47.81 and £195.19 a week better off in March 1981 prices.

But a further redistribution - again favouring higher income groups - has been brought about by the way in which the revenue was raised to finance these direct tax cuts. National Insurance contributions have been increased, partly to offset the reduction in the Exchequer subsidies, and a major increase in indirect taxation has been effected. Both these changes were regressive, and those cuts in public expenditure which have been effected to help finance the reduction in income tax have likewise reduced the living standards of households with children. The Thatcher government's fiscal redistribution to high income groups has not only signalled a new period of post-war politics, but has underlined, at a time when the hard Left calls for extra-parliamentary action, just how effective the parliamentary system can be in bringing about fundamental changes in the distribution of income and power in our society.

Policy issues in the distribution of income and wealth: some lessons from the Diamond Commission*

Dorothy Wedderburn

INTRODUCTION

The background to the establishment of the Royal Commission
on the Distribution of Income and Wealth in August 1974 was
political and was directly related to tensions surrounding the
attempts of successive governments to implement an incomes
policy. After the 1970 defeat of the Labour government dis-
content grew among the trade unions with the Conservative
government's legislation to control industrial relations and with
its particular versions of incomes policy. During this period in
opposition, the Labour Party began to work with the TUC on
the formulation of the 'social contract', which directed attention
to, among other things, inequalities in the distribution of income
and wealth. The February 1974 election manifesto of the Labour
Party spoke of the need for a Commission that would advise on
income distribution (earned and unearned) with particular
reference to differentials and job evaluation - that is still with
a flavour of incomes policy about it. In the event the Commission
was established after the Labour Party had been returned to
power 'to inquire into, and report on, such matters concerning
the distribution of personal incomes, both earned and unearned
and wealth, as may be referred to it by the government'. It
was given a standing reference (the full terms of which are
reproduced in the Appendix to this chapter) which invited an
analysis of the current position and past trends in the distribution of income and wealth.
  The preamble to the standing reference speaks of the need
for a comprehensive inquiry 'to help to secure a fairer distribution of income and wealth in the community'. Certainly, the
Commission was viewed generally, at that time, as a policy-
making body, and its activities appeared to be linked to such
declared Labour Party electoral intentions as 'to use taxation to

achieve a major redistribution of both wealth and income' and
'to introduce an annual tax on wealth above £100,000' and to
introduce a Capital Transfer Tax in place of estate duty (Labour
Party, 1974). The popular press described the Commission as
'a sort of time-bomb ticking away beneath the feet of the rich'
and the Confederation of British Industry, when presenting
evidence to the Commission in 1975, stated that the terms of
reference clearly prejudiced the outcome of any inquiries. Four
and a half years, and six reports later, it is doubtful whether
many ordinary people are aware of the Commission's continued
existence. Discussion of income and wealth redistribution has
largely disappeared from the political agenda; nothing has been
heard recently about a wealth tax; and the work of the Commission has received as much, if not more, criticism from the
Left as from the Right.

Yet this background may help to explain the choice of a
Royal Commission as the vehicle for the investigation of a subject which might be thought to be highly technical and yet is
politically charged. For Royal Commissions are supposed to be
chosen to represent the views of the 'man on the Clapham
omnibus' and this is usually seen to be achieved by a suitable
balance in the representation of different interest groups. In
the case of the Diamond Commission there is a full-time Chairman,
who was a former Labour Cabinet Minister, three members
representing financial and employing interests, two representing trade unions, and two or three academics with varying
amounts of professional interest and expertise in the area.

The Commission has its own staff, including economists and
statisticians, mainly on secondment from government departments. It co-operates with other government departments, who
have provided a lot of additional data to the extent that their
staffing position would allow. It has used consultants to prepare
special reports, and has drawn heavily on academic research
publications. The following is a personal account of my experi-
ences as a member of the Commission until August 1978.

The Chairman made it clear that in his view the task of the
Commission was to establish 'facts' and that all policy recommendations were to be eschewed. On receipt of a reference staff
would prepare a paper summarising sources and issues in relation to the reference. At this point the Commissioners became
involved in the crucial process of deciding what was a relevant
'fact' or question which we should attempt to answer and what
particular areas should be selected for a programme of work.
We would engage in a process of bargaining, which explains
why the reports show varying degrees of willingness to engage
in estimation on sensitive issues, and to pursue different topics
in depth. For example, Report No. 5 contains the results of a
model which was constructed in an attempt to investigate the
relationship between inherited and accumulated wealth (Report
No. 5, 1977, Ch. 9). Such a model clearly involves strong
assumptions about relationships between variables, as well as

estimates of values. But in another case, the Commission decided that it would not attempt to estimate the value of fringe benefits for higher incomes from employment, because, it argued, insufficient data was available, even though it was clear that such benefits were of considerable and increasing value at the top income levels.

The work proceeded with the staff returning to the Commission periodically with draft reports which would be discussed and amended in full meeting. At the same time the views of interested parties among the public would be solicited by advertisement, and the Commission would be involved in taking both oral and written evidence, from individuals and institutions. This evidence could range from expressions of strongly held opinions from employers, trade unions, or pressure groups through to evidence from economists on the use, say, of equivalence scales.

Three reports have been published so far on the standing reference, and three reports on specific references. The first of these was on income from dividends and its distribution, the second was on higher incomes from employment and the third was on lower incomes. Six background papers have also been published. [The Royal Commission was disbanded in July 1979, and in total it published five reports on the standing reference and three on specific references. The full list, together with the titles of the eight background papers, is reproduced in the bibliography under the heading Royal Commission.]

The reports which have emerged are a mine of information and are invaluable as references. To the policy-maker, however, they may appear baffling. Those issues which have been selected for discussion are not always obviously the most urgent, whilst others which are, by general agreement, both important and urgent, tend to become obscured beneath a mountain of statistical material. Since the Diamond Commission itself has shunned policy recommendations I will select a limited number of areas where, in my view, the reports do significantly add to our understanding of the processes which influence the distribution of resources in the UK.

SOME CHARACTERISTICS OF THE DATA PRODUCED

First a word about the nature of the data contained in the reports. It is impossible to describe fully the material contained in so many reports and background papers. I will select certain items for comment which will provide a general picture of the range of material to be found in the published reports on the standing reference.

Beginning with income, the reports bring together material published by a number of government departments, provide time series of varying length and successive reports up-date. For example, data on the dispersion of earnings are drawn from the

Department of Employment's now annual 'New Earnings Survey'
and from the Department of Health and Social Security's Statistics of Earnings. Distribution of household income is drawn from
the annual 'Family Expenditure Survey' of the Department of
Employment. This survey also forms the basis of the CSO's study
of the incidence of taxes and benefits on the distribution of
household income, which has been utilised by the Commission.
    The core data on the distribution of income relates to tax
units, and is obtained from Inland Revenue data, supplemented
by estimates supplied by the CSO to cover those units falling
below the tax threshold. Over the four years the Commission,
with the co-operation of Inland Revenue and other government
departments, has tackled certain deficiencies in these basic
statistics, for example excluding part-year income units, adding in an imputed rent for owner-occupiers, employees' superannuation contributions and other tax deductable items. The
tables provide some data on source of income, by income range,
and a separate distribution for tax units where the main earner
is economically active and inactive. But whilst the basic income
distribution, both before and after tax, is now available for
1949, 1954, 1959 and thereafter annually to 1974-5 [the latest
1976-7 in Report No. 7], the adjustments described above are
available, at most, for the years during which the Commission
has been working. Since some of these items, such as owner-
occupation and superannuation are likely to have been increasing in importance over time, it is still not possible to assess
their effect upon long-term trends.
    The Commission has been relatively conventional in its pre-
sentation of the statistics of income distribution, relying heavily
upon tables showing percentile shares. A special study of
international comparisons of personal income distribution was
commissioned (Background Paper No. 4, 1977). It proved
extremely difficult to obtain comparable data although that of
the best available quality was from consumer units in the UK,
USA and Canada for the 1970s. This suggested that the
distribution of incomes was more equal in the UK than in the
USA, with Canada being somewhat less unequal than the USA
(Report No. 5, 1977, p. 141. In the Background Paper No. 4,
chapter 3 compares available data for Canada and the UK).
Some studies of the income of particular groups under the
standing reference, e.g. of the self-employed and possibly of
women, are promised for the future. [Report No. 8 included
the study of the self employed but the study on women was
never finished or published.]
    When we turn to estimates of the distribution of wealth the
basic data are less complete because wealth is not at present
taxed in the UK although there are, of course, taxes on those
incomes derived from wealth and taxes on the transfer or
exchange of wealth (for example, estate duty and Capital Gains
Tax). The estate multiplier method as used by the Inland
Revenue in its own estimates of wealth distribution was the

starting point for the Commission's work. A number of academics
had experimented with methods for improving these official
estimates and the Commission benefited from their experience
(Atkinson, 1972; Atkinson and Harrison, 1974; Revell, 1967).
Thus, by first estimating personal sector balance sheets to
provide control totals, the Commission's estimates adjust for
(i) individuals excluded and (ii) wealth excluded or under-
valued by the estate duty method. These adjustments as made
by the Commission are only available for the years 1972-5. Most
of the wealth data relate to individuals, although some estimates
have been provided of the effect of marriage on the distribution,
on certain assumptions about the way in which couples are
paired in relation to their position in the wealth distribution
(Report No. 1, 1975, Table 40).

Another innovation was to extend the conventional Inland
Revenue definition of wealth to include the capitalised value of
occupational pension rights and the value of accrued rights to
state pensions. Again, however, these estimates are available
for only a limited number of years. In the fifth report separate
distributions and some average values are given for different
forms of wealth classified according to the degree of liquidity.
This also involves valuing marketable assets in terms of their
'realisation' or current sale values in contrast to the other
estimates which are based on 'going concern' values.

Some interesting exploration of the impact of changes in
relative asset prices upon the degree of inequality in the distribution of wealth have been reported. Finally a major exercise was undertaken, following earlier work by Harbury (1962),
to analyse a sample of wills which it was hoped would contribute
to an understanding of the role of inheritance in the distribution of wealth. Then on the basis of these findings, and using
a perpetual inventory method and certain simple demographic
assumptions, a model was constructed to study the relationship
between transmitted and accumulated wealth (Report No. 5,
1977, Chs 8 and 9).

Work is continuing to refine this model, and to include a model
of lifetime savings. A study on estates left by women by Professor Harbury (Harbury and Hitchens, 1977) was published in
the 'Economic Journal'. A number of other studies, including
an international comparison of wealth distribution and detailed
analysis of the ownership of two major assets, namely land and
company shares are under way. [A summary of the work on
international comparisons was published in Ch. 4 of Report
No. 7, 1979, and in more detail in Background Paper No. 7,
1979. Work on land was published in Report No. 7, 1979, as
was further information on company shares.]

THE DISTRIBUTION OF INCOME IN THE UK IN THE POST-WAR
PERIOD

The starting point for our discussion is the availability of a
consistent time series of income distribution for tax units (i.e.
a single person or a married couple with dependent children),
over a twenty-five-year period (both before and after direct
tax). The first notable feature is the small amount of change
that has occurred whatever measure is chosen. The share of the
lowest 50 per cent of tax units in the total of personal income
before tax was 23.7 per cent in 1949 and 24.2 per cent in
1974-5. After tax, it was 26.5 per cent in 1949 and 27.0 per
cent in 1974-5. Most change was registered by the top decile
group and within that the top 1 per cent. In 1949 the top 10
per cent of tax units received 33.2 per cent of total personal
income before tax and 26.6 per cent in 1974-5, a fall of approximately 20 per cent. But almost half of this decline occurred in
the six years at the beginning of the period, between 1949 and
1954. The after tax picture is similar, although the fall in the
share of the top decile group was less marked, from 27.1 per
cent in 1949 to 23.2 per cent in 1974-5 (Report No. 5, 1977,
Tables D1, D3). The Gini coefficient of the before tax distribution fluctuated. It fell from 41.1 per cent in 1949 to 38.8 in
1961. It rose again, and then fell from 1972-3 back to 37.1 in
1974-5.
   As early as 1962, Richard Titmuss had drawn attention to the
importance of taking account of social and demographic changes
when interpreting aggregate income distribution statistics,
although he himself made no attempt to estimate orders of magnitude (Titmuss, 1962). This task was undertaken by the Commission's staff with interesting results (a summary is available
in Report No. 5, 1977, Ch. 5, and a full account in Background
Paper No. 3, 1977). Using a technique of shift-share analysis,
the possible effects of four social and demographic changes
upon the personal income distribution (before direct taxes)
between 1951 and 1971, were explored. These were:

the pattern and extent of marriage;
the proportion of the population which is elderly;
the extent of female employment;
the proportion of the population in full-time education.

As conducted, the exercise is subject to important qualifications,
among which only two will be mentioned here. The first is the
assumption of a causal link running from the characteristics of
a population group to the income of that group. A good example
is the implied assumption about the levels of income of the
elderly, namely that because they are old they have low incomes.
The second is the assumed absence of any link running from
changes in the relative numbers of a population group to changes
in the income pattern of its members. For example, the method

implies that the reduction in the number of young entrants to
the labour force, resulting from an increase in young people
receiving full-time education, has no impact upon the wages of
those young who are in work.

The analysis suggests that over the twenty-year period in
question the four factors together would have made the income
distribution more unequal. As we have seen, however, there was
actually a small movement towards greater equality (as measured
by the Gini coefficient) and on further analysis it appears that
the fall in the share of the top decile group, which owed little
to the social and demographic changes being analysed, was more
than enough to outweigh any other trends. Within the bottom
90 per cent of the distribution, however, the shift share
analysis gives a forecast remarkably close to what actually
happened. Using once again the Gini coefficient as a summarising measure, inequality actually increased within the bottom
90 per cent of tax units. The analysis suggests that changes
in the extent of marriages (allowing for changes in the population structure), in the proportion of the population which is
elderly and the proportion of the population in full-time education, have all tended to make the distribution of income more
unequal; and although changes in the extent of female employment have tended to make it less unequal, the former tendencies
have outweighed the latter.

Such an approach to disaggregation of the income distribution
can be only a beginning. Not only is more sophisticated analysis
required, but more factors need to be isolated for study, particularly for policy purposes. For example, the policy implications
of an increase in the number of low income receivers arising
because more young people are receiving university education
will be viewed differently from that which results from an
increase in the number of single-parent families. But the usefulness of such analysis in directing attention to the interaction
of public policies in different spheres upon income distribution,
e.g. income maintenance for the elderly with educational policy,
as well as the importance of disaggregation for forecasting
future trends, is considerable. It certainly calls in question any
notion of unitary causation.

Returning now to examine the top of the income distribution,
two factors have to be encompassed. First, social and demographic changes appear to have had relatively little influence
upon trends at this level, and yet it is at the top that the most
marked change in shares, in a downward direction, can be
observed, over the post-war period. We noted above that the
fall in income share for the top decile was, in fact, largely
concentrated at the very top. The share of the top 1 per cent
of tax units in total personal income before tax fell from 11.2
per cent in 1949 to 6.2 per cent in 1974-5. In the light of these
spcial characteristics, a closer examination of the position of
these income groups and its implications for policy might well
have been expected, but it has so far not been undertaken

by the Commission. (Nor was such a study undertaken.)
None the less, some issues are worthy of discussion.

In many respects the top percentiles of the income distribution
appear to be unique. First, incomes at this level appear to be
derived from the combination of a number of different sources.
Income from self-employment is important, although until the
promised special study of this category it is not possible to be
precise. [Published in Report No. 8. 1979.] But so, too, is
investment income. In the 1970s it supplied a quarter of all
income before tax for the top 1 per cent of tax units and about
10 per cent for the next highest 2-5 per cent. Together the
top 5 per cent received more than a half of all investment
income accruing to persons. Around this level there appears
to be a qualitative change, for the next highest 5 per cent of
tax units received only 8 per cent of all investment income
which in turn contributed only 4 per cent of their total income.

It follows, then, that any special factors relating to movements
in investment income would be likely to have a differential
impact upon top income receivers. To begin with it should be
noted that the estimates of the share of total personal income
derived from investment is difficult to reconcile with the global
national income estimates. It is also clear that personal ownership of company securities has been declining over this period
(in favour of institutions), and possibly even the share of
personal wealth in total national wealth. More particularly,
income from dividends in real terms has not increased in line
with other sources of income. The significance of such changes
for the total economic position of top income receivers relative
to the rest of the population is far from clear, however.

Tax avoidance has also probably increased over the post-war
period and with British tax laws this is known to be most
readily available to those with self-employment income, either as
a main or a subsidiary source, and investment income. This same
period has also seen the growth in another form of tax avoidance
for those with employment incomes, namely the cluster of benefits such as occupational pensions, company cars, and low
interest company loans, private medical insurance, etc. It is
not suggested that these are confined to the top end of the
income distribution, but they are undoubtedly of far greater
importance in value terms and degree of concentration there.
The Commission's Report on Higher Incomes from Employment
showed that at the higher levels of employment incomes the cost
to the employer (as distinct from value to the employee, which
is very different) could be as much as 25 to 30 per cent of
average salary. (Report No. 3, 1976, ch. 4 and Appendix H.)
There is evidence to suggest that one effect of more recent
incomes policies has been to increase this trend. Thus we have
a situation where the income distribution, as conventionally
measured, may be misleading because the *form* in which remuneration is received, and command over resources is obtained, has
changed over time.

A number of stages of incomes policy pursued by successive governments in the post war period could have been expected to have a particular effect at the top end of the income distribution. From April 1973 to July 1974 there were limits on the total amount of increase that could be paid to an individual. From July 1975 to 1976 no increases at all were allowable for those earning £8,500 or more a year, and from July 1976-7 there was again an upper limit upon individual increases. The statistics available from the Commission cover only the first of these limitations, but there does not appear to be any discontinuity in the trend at the top of the distribution. This suggests that other factors, either the ability to circumvent incomes policy by changes in the form of remuneration or by other means, e.g. change of job title, or the relatively greater importance of other sources of income at these levels, are at play to offset any effect which might otherwise be felt.

From the viewpoint of the policy-maker, the top end of the income distribution is a politically sensitive one. It is unfortunate, therefore, that the global statistics of distribution provide so little guidance to the underlying economic and social trends.

It is not only at the top end of the distribution, however, that incomes policies have apparently had little effect. The general stability in the overall income distribution suggests that this is a more general phenomenon, yet one which must cause concern to some government policy-makers. There is no doubt that certain phases of incomes policy have been looked to, not only to improve relatively the position of the low paid, but also to reduce the dispersion at the top. (For example, in the period July 1975 - July 1976 increases of £6 a week for all except those earning £8,500 a year, for whom no increase at all was allowed.) But even if we concentrate upon the data on the distribution of individual earnings, the evidence for a narrowing of relativities here is by no means obvious. The Department of Employment's 'New Earnings Survey' provides a series over the period 1970-6. Admittedly, there was some narrowing of the distribution, slightly more for men than women, but it was by no means concentrated in periods of incomes policy, and the trend was actually reversed in that period 1975-6, when it might have been expected to be most marked (Dean, 1978).

Expressed as a percentage of the median, gross weekly earnings of full-time adult male employees in the lowest decile increased from 65.4 in 1970 to 68.1 in 1977 and in the highest decile fell from 160.6 to 157.7 in 1977, but within the period a narrowing and a subsequent widening of relativities were both observable. The most marked and consistent contraction was the reduction in the highest percentile earnings of non-manual men which fell from 349.6 of the median in 1970 to 291.9 in 1976 irrespective of the form of incomes policy (Report No. 5, 1977, Table 18. These would be incomes of £11,000 a year upwards in 1976). This is not to say that differentials within companies, for example, have not been disturbed by the

operation of these policies, but in the aggregate there is little
evidence 'that there has been a strong compression of pay
brought about directly by incomes policies' (Dean, 1978, p. 48).

When considering the likely influence of such changes upon
the aggregate income distribution for tax units, allowance has
to be made for other factors, such as the presence of second
earners and these, we know, have increased. The activity ratio
of married women in the age group 25–59 more than doubled
between 1951 and 1971 (from 23.7 per cent to 49.3 per cent),
and the percentage of tax units with earning wives increased
over all the decile groups of the distribution. This also encom-
passes the period when women's pay has been strongly influenced by the movement towards equal pay, generally allowed as
an exception to statutory pay limits. Another factor is the
possibility of increasing numbers of people (men and women)
with second jobs, an area about which all too little is known.
Thus what is happening to the content of men's pay packets is
by no means the only important factor influencing the position
of tax units in the middle of the income distribution.

Indeed, one of the most noticeable developments of the last
twenty years is the weakening of the links between individual
gross earnings and the real standard of living which is available
to any particular family grouping. If we ignore the fact that
the standard of living of particular families will vary according
to family composition, not only is the earning power of a wife
an important economic fact, but there has also been an increased
direct tax burden felt by most decile groups over the period.
The average rate of income tax more than doubled in the period
1959 to 1974–5 for the bottom 90 per cent of the distribution,
whereas that of the top decile group increased by less than a
quarter. In 1959 the top 1 per cent of tax units paid 34.5 per
cent of all personal income tax, whereas in 1974–5 they paid
only 15.8 per cent (Report No. 5, 1977, Table 7).

There have also been other influences upon the real standard
of living, not immediately encompassed by data either on individual earnings or by the aggregate income distribution. The
report on Lower Incomes discussed briefly the possibility of
differential effects of inflation upon families at different income
levels, of particular importance in a five-year period when the
Retail Price index doubled (Report No. 6, 1978, p. 6 and
Appendix F). Moreover, as we noted above, fringe benefits
are by no means confined to top income receivers, and yet
their incidence at other levels is extremely uneven as between
manual and non-manual occupations, men and women, between
industries and between sectors. Thus it can be concluded that,
the link between any single individual's pay or salary and the
real command over resources that he or she enjoys is becoming
increasingly opaque.

THE PROBLEM OF POVERTY - THE LOWER INCOMES
REFERENCE

If policy implications were to be spelled out by the Commission
anywhere, they might have been expected in the reference on
lower incomes (interpreted as about the bottom 25 per cent of
the distribution) (see Appendix for full terms of reference).
Yet once again the emphasis in this report was upon factual
analysis, even though the Commission did allow itself to
address the question of whether personal characteristics associated with earning capacity are determined genetically (Report
No. 6, 1978, p. 149). Perhaps not surprisingly it found the
evidence inconclusive, although an addendum signed by three
Commissioners, asserted that 'the genetic argument contributes
nothing to an understanding of the causes of lower incomes in
contemporary society' (Report No. 6, 1978, p. 157).
The Lower Incomes report is the only one which has so far
tried to make allowance for differences in the size and composition of tax units and families. A considerable amount of evidence
was received about equivalence scales which explored both the
debatable nature of some of the assumptions underlying their
construction as well as the practical difficulties involved. In the
end, the Commission adopted the scales laid down as the supplementary benefit scale rates, which are used to calculate entitlement to income support from the Supplementary Benefits Commission. The argument used was that these particular scales
embodied a view taken by parliament as to the relative need of
different groups and, moreover, the results did not differ
radically from those yielded by more sophisticated methods.
Unlike the reports on the standing reference, the Lower Incomes
Reference and its accompanying background paper (Background
Paper No. 5, 1978) made primary use of the income data from
the Family Expenditure Survey which has certain deficiencies
(It is obtained from a continuous sample survey where it is
known that there is response bias, in particular that self-
employment and investment income are under-reported.)
The Lower Incomes report found, perhaps not surprisingly,
that about 60 per cent of the families in the lower part of the
equivalent income distribution relied almost exclusively upon
state benefits, and they comprised the usual disadvantaged
groups, the elderly, the disabled and long-term sick, one-
parent families and the unemployed (an increasingly important
category since the mid 1960s when the employment situation
worsened and both the numbers, and the length of period
unemployed, have increased). The relative position of the
lower income group in aggregate, and the separate distributions
within groups of families of different size and composition,
remained remarkably stable. Over a ten-year period the income
share of the lowest quarter was only about 12 per cent of the
total compared with 44 per cent going to the top quarter. The
real value of lower incomes (measured by their purchasing power

in constant prices after taxes) grew by about 40 per cent, in
line with GNP, until 1974 followed by a fall in 1975 and 1976
when GNP also fell. This is not surprising given the basic
structure of the social security system where, in recent years,
a statutory link has been established between certain national
insurance benefits and movements both in earnings and prices.
At the same time, the system has become much more complex in
operation and more varied in its impact. The elderly have done
relatively better than other groups, and the short-term unemployed are protected by earnings related supplements. On the
other hand, the long-term unemployed, or any other dependent
families where there are children, are badly off and the evidence suggests that here incomes are barely adequate. [Changes
in policy since 1979 have broken the link between benefits and
earnings.]

   The intensive discussion over this period of the position of
the poor and the frequent revision of levels of benefit have
served to ensure that those excluded from the labour market
should at least share in the increase in the real standard of living
of the rest of the community. But a number of other influences
are at work to prevent them improving their relative position.
First, there is the interaction between levels of pay and benefit,
which derives from what some people see as the possible disincentive effects of benefit levels creeping close to or above
earnings levels. Second, benefit levels have improved in relation to net earnings after tax (as the tax burden has risen,
see above). But the need for a large tax yield has itself been
influenced by such factors as the increasing proportion of the
elderly in the population and the increasing number of unemployed. It is also possible that families at the bottom of the
distribution have not improved their position relative to families
around the median because the contribution of working wives
has increased the average after tax income. Certainly, the
policy-maker needs a clearer understanding of the multiplicity
of factors which have been at work here. Some policy comments
were made forcibly by the authors of the background paper,
'The Causes of Poverty'. They argued that if the existing
complex system of income support which exists for the working
poor (consisting of child benefit, family income supplement,
etc.) could be made automatic 'the living standards of the working poor and also of the non-working poor could within limits
be set at whatever level society chose' (Background Paper No. 5,
1978, p. 134). Their interesting analysis also suggests, somewhat controversially, that poverty does not stem from low pay.
The reason is that most of those on the lowest pay (in terms of
hourly earnings) are married women whose earnings ensure
that their families are not among the poorest, whilst the poorest
workers are men with large families, whose earnings may be
good but still inadequate in relation to their need. Among
families with earnings, whether a wife works is a crucial determinant of whether a family is financially speaking poor.

THE DISTRIBUTION OF WEALTH IN THE UK IN THE POST-WAR
PERIOD

The Commission has not yet produced a combined distribution
of income and wealth, although it is investigating the links
between the two. [No information was subsequently published.]
Nevertheless we can deduce from the existing data that there
is a heavy concentration of wealth ownership among those at
the top end of the income distribution. Among the many difficulties in analysing the relationship further is the fact that
the presently available statistics on the distribution of wealth
take the individual as the unit of analysis, whereas the income
distribution relates to tax units. Moreover, the quality of the
wealth statistics is much poorer and greater caution in interpreting them is therefore needed. None the less it is reasonable
to say that wealth is far more unevenly distributed than income
in the UK. On the best available evidence, so far, in 1975 the
top 1 per cent of wealth-holders owned a quarter of all personal
wealth and the top 20 per cent owned 78 per cent (1 per cent
here is approximately 400,000 individuals). The average value
of the wealth held by the top 1 per cent was £135,000. (These
estimates are on the basis of market valuation, Report No. 5,
1977, Table 45.) The evidence generally supports the view that
there has been a trend towards greater equality of wealth-
holding over the very long run, as well as in the last fifteen
years. But the precise significance of this trend, as well as its
causes remains somewhat obscure. Commenting on the long run
series, from just before the First World War up to 1960, Tony
Atkinson noted that although the share of the top 1 per cent
of wealth-holders declined, the share of the next 4 per cent
actually increased, and he suggested that this might reflect 'in
part the rearrangement of wealth within families rather than the
redistribution between rich and poor families' (estimates from
Revell quoted in Report No. 1, 1975, Table 41. See also Atkinson, 1972, p. 24). One factor inducing such a rearrangement
would be the incidence of estate duty tax.
    In the longest consistent series available in the Commission's
own report, from 1960 to 1975 (which is based on the assumption that individuals excluded from the Inland Revenue statistics
have no wealth), the share of the top 1 per cent of individuals
is shown as falling from 38.2 per cent in 1960 to 27.6 per cent
in 1974 and 23.2 per cent in 1975. The share of the next 4 per
cent in this period shows some small year-to-year fluctuations,
but is basically stable around a quarter. The bottom 80 per
cent of the distribution shows the most marked change, but only
at the very end of the period. In 1960 and 1972 the bottom 80
per cent are shown as owning 10 per cent of personal wealth
and this has only risen to 13.6 per cent in 1973, although by
1975 it is 18.2 per cent (Report No. 5, 1977, Table 33, and for
the alternative series referred to below, Table 39). An alternative series provided by the Commission for four years

(1972-5) is based on an alternative assumption that individuals
excluded from the Inland Revenue's own estimates have positive
wealth-holdings. This has the effect of increasing the share of
wealth attributed to the bottom 80 per cent of the distribution,
but the trends over time remain similar. Methods of improving
the estimates of wealth distribution, particularly at this lower
end, are badly needed, and the Commission has considered the
possibility of conducting a survey of wealth by means of personal interviews with a random sample of the population in
order to supplement Inland Revenue tax data [see paragraph
4.57 of Report No. 7, 1979, for the outcome of this exercise].
So long as such heavy reliance has to be based upon somewhat
arbitrary assumptions it is difficult, for example, to provide
any finer estimates of ownership by decile shares at the lower
end of the distribution or to begin to analyse the composition
of wealth at such levels. It has been widely assumed, for
example, that the extension of owner-occupation (from 25.9
per cent of wealth-owners in 1960 to 43.8 per cent in 1975) has
been an important influence making for more equality in the
distribution (Report No. 5, 1977, Table 72). But the trend to
increased home ownership has been fairly steady over the whole
period and can scarcely have affected the fairly sharp increase
in the share of the bottom 80 per cent which was shown between
1974 and 1975. It seems likely that the influence of home ownership has been most marked in the middle ranges of the distribution and that there remain substantial numbers of individuals
with no or very little wealth at all.

Not only is there heavy concentration in the ownership of
wealth but the characteristics of the largest estates are very
different from the smaller ones. Estates whose total value was
£200,000 or more in 1975 consisted predominantly of listed shares
and other company securities (over one-third), of land (17 per
cent) and of dwellings (12 per cent). Individuals with estates
worth more than £100,000 owned nearly half of all shares in
private hands and 46 per cent of all land. In the lower ranges
of wealth the predominant form was dwellings (over a half) and
life policies (about a fifth) (Report No. 5, 1977, Tables 29 and
30). These marked differences in the type of asset held at
different levels of wealth makes the year to year estimates of
the degree of concentration by total value particularly suscept-
ible to fluctuations in the relative price of different assets. The
value of company shares has been volatile but has increased
less than the retail price index, while the price of land and
dwellings has shown a more rapid rate of increase than other
prices. Indeed, even allowing for the increased incidence of
owner-occupation, it is notable that the share of physical assets
in total personal wealth increased from 30 per cent in 1960 to
54 per cent in 1975 while that of shares and securities declined
from 23 per cent to 9.6 per cent.

Independent evidence that this decline in the importance of
shares and securities in the total of personal wealth-holding

may represent more than a relative fall in price, but also a fall
in quantity is given by the estimates which show that the proportion of listed UK ordinary company shares held by persons
has fallen from 56 per cent in 1963 to 40 per cent in 1975
(Erritt and Alexander, 1977). Correspondingly, the proportions
held by financial companies and institutions has risen from 30
per cent to 48 per cent.

This kind of change emphasises the necessity for setting the
total of personal wealth-holding in the wider context of national
wealth and this the CSO has begun to do (with encouragement
from the Royal Commission). The first estimates suggest that
not only has personal wealth declined as a percentage of total
national wealth, but also as a multiple of personal income.

> In 1966 the net wealth of 'households' was about 3.5 times
> total personal income and accounted for three quarters of
> the total national wealth: in 1976 it is estimated to have been
> 2.9 times total personal income, and whereas an accurate
> estimate of national wealth is not yet available, it seems
> possible that the corresponding proportion of total national
> wealth may turn out to be about a half. ('Economic Trends',
> 1978)

There is much interest in unravelling further the interconnec-
tions between the volume and nature of wealth-holding of persons, financial institutions, companies and government so that
it is possible better to understand the new forms of relationship
which appear to be developing between ownership and control,
and the new role, in the functioning of the economy, of personal
wealth-holdings.

The Commission produced estimates of wealth extended to
include the value of accrued rights in the state pension scheme.
The use of this wider definition reduces dramatically the degree
of inequality in the wealth distribution. Not only is the total
of personal wealth increased substantially (from £238 billion to
£392 billion) but the sum is distributed among all adults varying
only with age and sex. The Commission discussed at length the
need for using alternative definitions of both income and wealth,
but the usefulness of this particular exercise is very doubtful
(Report No. 5, 1977, ch. 2). In the UK the state pension scheme
is unfunded, an individual's entitlement cannot be realised in
any way until the conditions for receiving the pension have been
fulfilled, and, moreover, the nature of entitlement is subject to
change by political fiat. If wealth is held to be economically and
socially important because: 'apart from providing a source of
income which is compatible with a life of leisure, wealth gives
opportunity, security, social power, influence and independence'
(Meade, 1978), then £6,000 of capital attributed to a woman
aged 50-54, as the value of her rights in the state scheme, is
qualitatively different from £6,000 which she may have invested
in a building society. Rights in occupational pension funds are

clearly in an intermediate category between more conventional
forms of wealth and state pensions. But here we encounter wide
variations in the incidence and characteristics of such pensions,
between occupations, industries and between men and women.
From the viewpoint of the policy-maker, therefore, the need
for more disaggregation of the wealth estimates by personal
characteristics as well as according to the degree of market-
ability of the assets owned emerges as an important consideration.

The idea that inherited wealth may be considered a fit object
for taxation, since it is in the nature of a windfall compared
with that wealth accumulated out of lifetime income as a result
of effort and thrift, has long influenced taxation policy in the
UK and led the Commission, as we noted above, to devote some
of its resources to make some estimates of the order of magnitude of inherited and accumulated wealth. These were based on
extremely restricted assumptions and were published with a
view to encouraging research workers to become interested in
some of the problems associated with the construction of the
model (Report No. 5, 1977, ch. 9). But the study of the pattern
of inheritance based on an analysis of a random sample of wills
receiving probate in 1973, and which formed part of the model,
produced some interesting results. It found that, irrespective
of size, the great bulk of property is bequeathed to relatives
(from 90 per cent in the smaller estates to 75 per cent in larger
ones). But there is a significant fragmentation of wealth on
death, the average number of bequests increasing from five in
the smaller estates to twenty-four in the larger ones, while
larger estates also tend to be more equally distributed. We
cannot deduce from this anything about the effect upon inequality in the ownership of wealth because we know nothing, for
example, about gifts inter vivos, about the extent to which the
inheritors may receive bequests from a number of sources or
about the effects of inheritance upon the ability to accumulate.
For those who are interested in the analysis of the effect of
wealth ownership upon life-chances, this material is disappoint-
ing because even the expectation of inheritance may suffice to
enhance opportunities and extend the range of temporal choices.
However, it is a small beginning in an area which calls for
further study.

CONCLUSION

In discussing some of the policy implications of the Diamond
Commission I have not attempted to specify what policies or
which policy-makers. What is not in the reports, as much as
what they contain, underlines the complexity of the interaction
of demographic, social and economic factors which generate the
distribution and control of resources in an economy like the
UK. It might, however, be thought surprising that I have

omitted any specific discussion of the fiscal implications or indeed the consequences of fiscal policy for the distribution of resources. This is done deliberately not only because I am not equipped for such a discussion, or because such a discussion would require another paper; it is also because a major debate about the chaotic nature of the present UK tax structure has been initiated by the publication of the Meade report (Meade, 1978). This contains proposals for a 'new Beveridge scheme' for dealing with the so-called poverty trap and other deficiencies in the existing social security system, which occupied much of the discussion of the Commission in its sixth report. It also advocates a progressive expenditure tax system combined with 'a system of progressive taxation on wealth with some discrimination against inherited wealth' (Meade, 1978, p. 518).

But for a successful outcome to that discussion as well as for providing answers to the major questions still left unanswered by Diamond, priority should be given to unravelling the generation of original income, and here to the interplay of economic and political factors such as ownership and control, with social factors such as the importance of custom and convention in determining levels of remuneration. (For some evidence of the role of custom and convention, see Report No. 3, 1976, ch. 8).

APPENDIX: THE TERMS OF REFERENCE AND PUBLICATIONS OF THE ROYAL COMMISSION ON THE DISTRIBUTION OF INCOME AND WEALTH

Standing reference
To help to secure a fairer distribution of income and wealth in the community there is a need for a thorough and comprehensive enquiry into the existing distribution of income and wealth. There is also a need for a study of past trends in that distribution and for regular assessments of the subsequent changes.

The government therefore ask the Commission to undertake an analysis of the current distribution of personal income and wealth and of available information on past trends in that distribution and would welcome an initial report on this as early as possible during the first year of the Commission's operation, and subsequent reports from time to time.

These reports should cover personal incomes at all levels; earned income of all kinds (including fringe and non-monetary benefits); unearned income of all kinds; capital gains; and all forms of personal wealth. They should take into account the incidence of taxation and any other factor which the Commission may consider relevant. Report No. 1, 1975; Report No. 4, 1976; Report No. 5, 1977; Report No. 7, 1979; Report No. 8, 1979.

Income from companies and its distribution
The Government therefore ask the Commission to prepare a

report, based on the most reliable information available to them and drawing on material assembled under their standing reference, on:

(i)   the pattern of distribution of ownership of equity capital capital and of income arising from it between United Kingdom pension funds, life insurance funds, other institutions, companies, individuals resident in the United Kingdom and overseas recipients. The Commission are asked to show as far as possible the final distribution of the income to individuals of different income levels in the United Kingdom and the trends in distribution over a recent period of years;

(ii)   the pattern of financing of United Kingdom companies, including financing by equity and non-equity capital; and in particular the role of dividends in the raising of capital which does not have to be remunerated by a fixed return for the financing of long term investment. The Commission are asked to distinguish as far as possible the significance of equity capital and dividends for companies of different sizes, sectors and rates of growth;

(iii)   changes over a recent period of years in the total of dividends paid by companies in the United Kingdom covered by dividend control, and in the capital in relation to which those dividends were paid; and the relationship in a similar illustrative period between the growth of different forms of personal income, including dividends, other investment income and income from employment and self-employment. The Commission are asked to take into account capital gains and losses where practicable and appropriate;

(iv)   such further information as would in the Commission's view be directly relevant to the Government's review.

Report No. 2, 1975.

Higher incomes from employment
The Government therefore ask the Commission:

(i)   to analyse the present position and past trends in the levels and distribution of such incomes, including all forms of monetary and non-monetary benefit, and showing separately the incidence of taxation and of changes in the value of money;

(ii)   to include in their analysis directors' fees; remuneration for part-time employment at comparable rates; and returns on personal investment insofar as these can be regarded as a form of remuneration arising from the employment or self-employment;

(iii)   to examine the economic and social reasons given for the levels and distribution of such incomes in relation to others, including for example the degrees of personal responsibility and risk; the qualifications, experience, ability and individual effort required; the international as well as domestic market for certain occupations; and such other factors as the Commission may consider relevant.

Report No. 3, 1976.

Lower incomes
There is a need for a comprehensive and objective analysis of incomes at the lower levels (say about the lowest 25 per cent of income recipients).

The Government therefore ask the Commission:
(i)   to analyse the present position in the levels and distribution of such incomes from all sources before and after tax, in relation not only to individuals but also to households and families;
(ii)   to analyse past trends in such incomes and in particular trends over the past five years;
(iii)   to examine the economic, social and other factors which give rise to low incomes, both inclusive and exclusive of incomes derived from social security benefits.

The government would welcome a progress report within one year.

Report No. 6, 1978.

NOTE

*Paper presented at the Conference on Canadian Incomes, Winnipeg, 10-12 May 1979, sponsored by the Economic Council of Canada. It was written before the Commission was disbanded in July 1979, before the publication of Reports 7 and 8. It has only been updated by brief references in brackets in the text.

The taxation of agricultural wealth: Northfield and after*

Alister Sutherland

The average full-time farmer has a net worth of at least one-
third of a million pounds. For products which are often in
surplus, he enjoys under the umbrella of the CAP a degree of
protection against world competition greater than that aspired
to by our manufacturing industries. He has a set of tax reliefs
which is exceeded by no other business man, and in some
respects, not least total relief from local authority rates, and
profit averaging, exceeds them. He enjoys also the benefits of
exceptional government support. In addition to capital grants,
the Ministry of Agriculture, Fisheries and Food (MAFF) supplies
the services of about 13,400 civil servants. (The Department of
Industry has 9,120.) As there are about 126,000 full-time
farms, there is one civil servant for every nine of them.
    Yet the agricultural lobby invariably claims that 'the capital
intensity' of agriculture is so high, mainly because of high land
prices, that capital taxes, despite the large existing reliefs,
are a serious threat. That is said to be so because farmers'
incomes, despite the Common Agricultural Policy (CAP), tax
relief, and government support, have been so low (for is not
'the yield' on agricultural land very 'low') that payment of
Capital Transfer Tax (CTT) could only be accomplished by the
sale of the farm - or some of it - leading to 'a fragmentation of
holdings', which in turn is alleged to produce losses in farm
efficiency.
    Although that was not the main intention, the alleged potential
impact of especially CTT on the working farmer produced some
of the main farming submissions to the Northfield Commission -
and invoked the most powerful expressions of oral remonstrance
at the public meetings held by that Committee. Although they
fell well short of the demands made by the National Farmers'
Union (NFU) and Country Landowners Association (CLA), the
Committee did recommend some further reliefs. In general line

with these conclusions, in the 1980 budget the Chancellor made
no new concessions to farmers, other than the general one raising the starting point for CTT to £50,000; but the government
review of capital taxation continued, as did the lobbying. In
the 1981 budget the general impact of CTT was greatly reduced;
and special major concessions were made to agricultural landlords. The deficiencies in both the farming case for further
special treatment, and in the Northfield Committee's handling
of that case, remain very relevant to current policy. The following pages first outline and criticise what Northfield did and
this is followed by an analysis in some depth of the weaknesses
of the farming case. The 1981 budgetary changes are then set
out in more detail.

THE NORTHFIELD COMMITTEE

The Committee of Inquiry into the Acquisition and Occupancy
of Agricultural Land was set up in September 1977 by the then
Minister of Agriculture, The Rt. Hon. John Silkin MP, and it
reported in July 1979 (Northfield, 1979). The terms of reference
were 'to examine recent trends in agricultural land acquisition
and occupancy as they affect the structure of the agricultural
industry'. The Chairman was Lord Northfield, formerly Donald
Chapman, the Labour MP for Birmingham, Northfield. The
great majority of the Committee represented a variety of agricultural interests. I was the specialist economist adviser to
the Committee from 1977 until I resigned, after prolonged and
basic disagreements about the analysis and contents of the
report, in March 1979.
   Despite the groundswell of agricultural opinion, the Committee found in fact that financial institutions (pension funds,
insurance companies, etc.) owned only about 1.2 per cent of
all agricultural land; and that such institutions were currently
buying about 10 per cent of the land offered for sale. (For the
details, see the useful Appendix V by Dr Richard Munton.)
Much of this was 'let land', so if an institution bought land from
an individual landlord the actual farming continued to be done
by the same tenant. (As well as having had - since 1948 -
security of tenure for his own lifetime, an agricultural tenant
since 1976 has had the right to hand on the tenancy, without
any liability to Capital Transfer Tax, to two future generations
of 'eligible successors'.) The Committee also concluded (para.
333)

> that, in the market for let land, the activities of the financial
> institutions give a push to prices especially when the market
> is rising. There is, however, no evidence that they are
> responsible for high prices in the vacant possession market,
> where the major purchasers appear to be neighbouring far-
> mers extending their holdings.

The Committee recommended that institutional purchases should be monitored; but found no case for restraints.

Overseas buyers, again contrary to prior agricultural impressions, were estimated to own only about 1 per cent of the land, a good deal of which would be of poor quality, bought for sporting or investment purposes. The Committee recommended no immediate action; but suggested that there should be 'reserve powers'.

The Committee wanted there to be enough new and young blood to enter the industry. Entry was difficult because of (a) 'the high cost of establishment as an owner-occupier'; coupled with (b) 'the shortage of tenancies'. Analysis of the evidence shows that for (a) the price of vacant possession land is established by existing farmers, and not by the institutions and the foreigner, who were postulated as very willing to pay more than 'the agricultural value' of the land. Farmers are prepared to pay a high price when buying additional land precisely because they are well informed about the prospects for farm income, and because of the considerable advantages that this form of investment has for working farmers. The prospects for capital gain are great (and there is roll-over relief for Capital Gains Tax (CGT)); and the working farmer relief for CTT (see below) would not apply to additional investment by farmers in non-business assets. Since the Committee was not prepared to contemplate any reduction in these advantages for existing farmers, but only to increase them, it follows that the 'difficulty of entry' can only increase, since the reason for the difficulty is the high price of land, which is determined by the well informed activities of existing farmers.

As to (b), 'the shortage of tenancies' there are two main causes for this. First, there is the protection given to the existing tenants, and to their two eligible successors. This exceptional security of tenure for three generations, plus the brake on rent increases exerted by the arbitration machinery of the Agricultural Holdings Act 1948, are factors explaining why tenanted land typically sells in the market for 40 per cent less than land with vacant possession. Since the Committee was prepared to recommend only minor changes to the heritability of tenancies (see para. 623 onwards), that reason for the 'shortage' will undoubtedly continue to operate. The second reason is the substantially greater tax concessions offered to working farmers, i.e. owner-occupiers, as compared to the landlord owners of tenanted land. Thus for capital tax the landlord did not at that time enjoy the agricultural/business relief of a 50 per cent valuation reduction for CTT; and he had to pay interest if he opted to pay his CTT on land by instalments. (The 1981 budget introduced a new valuation relief of 20 per cent and also extended interest free instalments to him; see p. 111). For income tax purposes, agricultural rents, like urban rents, dividends and other forms of unearned income, are treated as investment income, and therefore are subject to

the surcharge if big enough. This means that where he is
fortunate enough to have a tenancy die out without eligible
successors, the landlord will gain not only from the 40 per cent
or so increase in the value of his land now that he has vacant
possession, but also from his access to working farmer tax
relief on both income and capital. Thus the landlord has very
great monetary incentives not to grant another tenancy, but
instead to take in hand and farm himself, i.e. put in a manager,
rather than another tenant. A large majority of the Committee,
rightly in my view, was not prepared to recommend that agricultural landlords should in future be given the same tax
concessions as working farmers. Nor was a majority of the Committee (paras 684-9) prepared to take the alternative route for
reducing the difference between landlords and owner-occupiers
by recommending that some of the fiscal concessions to working
farmers should be reduced, for example by restoring some
effective upper size limit, based on the evidence about the
acreage above which efficiency ceases to increase - see below.
The Committee was thus resolute in failing to recommend anything effective to reduce 'the shortage of tenancies' about which
it professed such concern.

That concern was, however, itself not based on anything more
substantial than a piece of circular reasoning. At para. 579 we
read:

> We emphasise in our second objective [para. 19b] that we
> want to see a continued variety of forms of tenure; the let
> sector, by its very existence, supplies an important part
> of this and has a major role to play in British agriculture.
> We therefore conclude that there is a good case for retain-
> ing a healthy reasonably substantial let sector.

This could be more tersely expressed as 'we want there to be a
let sector because that is what we have said we want'. The evidence, on the other hand, was that no one has yet demonstrated
that in general tenanted land is farmed either more or less
efficiently than owner-occupied land; that is not in itself surprising, since more land is farmed by those whose holding
consists of both owned and rented land than by any other
category of farmer. Nor has anyone shown that having a pension
fund or insurance company as landlord produces results which
are different from having a non-institutional personal landlord.
In any event, in order to 'preserve the let sector' it is not
necessary to 'preserve the private landlord.' A sale of let land
to an institution leaves the tenant (and his two eligible successors) in occupation. And an institution has somewhat less
financial incentive to take in hand than a private landlord,
should that chance arise. Since it cannot be shown that either
the type of ownership or the type of occupant makes any difference to farming output or farming efficiency, why should
any disinterested party accept the Committee's a priori commit-

ment to the conclusion that there should be an attempt, at the general taxpayer's expense, to stem 'the decline of the let sector'?

In order to 'mitigate the pressures on private landlords so that the rate of decline can be steadied' (para. 37), the Committee concluded that:

> while some of us would support major changes, most of us could only go along with more modest measures such as a degree of indexation for CTT and CGT; extending the payments period for CTT; some deferment of CGT for lifetime transfers within a family; setting landlords' management charges against income tax; recovery of VAT on repairs and maintenance on let land; and some changes to the rules for Maintenance Funds. (para. 38)

It can be calculated that to extend for landlords the period for paying CTT by instalments from eight to ten years (with interest then at 6 per cent for a transfer at death, and on the assumption of an inflation rate of 10 per cent and a discount rate of 10 per cent) would effectively have reduced the landlords' tax bill by about 11 per cent. The value of the other tax concessions recommended for landlords was not quantified either, but would have been not inconsiderable. They would certainly have had an impact on equity, reducing it both horizontally (agricultural landlords would do better than those who owned other types of assets, for instance gilt-edged securities, equities or urban property) and vertically (agricultural landlords would do better than those with no assets). What these concessions would not do is to be big enough to prevent any landlord who could from taking back his land – see the arguments above. Thus the main positive recommendations of the Committee are directed to securing objectives ('preserving the let sector') which have not been shown to be desirable, using methods which would not work.

For owner-occupiers, the case put forward with great vigour by the farming establishment may be epitomised by a quotation from the National Farmers' Union in 1979: 'We consider that the *drastic* reduction in the level of Capital Transfer Tax is necessary if *serious* damage to the structure of the agricultural industry is to be avoided' (my italics). (As well as continuing to press for additional CTT reliefs for owner-occupier farmers, the NFU, as well as the CLA, is in favour of extending favourable working farmer treatment to landlords, i.e. to non-working farmers.) However, the evidence when properly analysed, as shown below, demonstrated quite the reverse. That is, CTT with the working farmer concessions, and the better known tax avoidance devices, had been so watered down that it posed no threat to agriculture, and that was so even before the major further general reduction of 1981. Rather, the main argument advanced to justify the existing level of concessions – the alleged great importance of economies of scale throughout the

whole range of farm sizes, without limit - does no such thing.
Some increases in the 1980 effective rate of CTT for farmers
would have no adverse effects on agricultural output or agricultural efficiency. The Committee floundered with the implications of this evidence. However, although it did not even
attempt to make a case that it was either necessary or desirable
(see para. 687), the Committee did recommend that owner-
occupiers also should benefit from an extension of the time to
pay CTT from eight years to ten years, while in their case
retaining the concession of paying no interest. (Assuming 10
per cent inflation and 10 per cent discount rate, that would
mean reducing the effective tax bill by about 13 per cent - see
below.) In addition the Committee recommended for owner-
occupiers indexation for both CTT and CGT.

In the end, although the information collected about institu-
tions and foreign land holdings is useful, the Northfield
Committee had no clear or defensible set of objectives; and the
Report has fundamental analytical flaws.

SHOULD FARMING HAVE TAX EXEMPTIONS?

The main purpose of CTT is the equitable one of continuing the
slow process of reducing the inequality of wealth. The average
full-time farmer is in the top 1 per cent of owners of marketable
wealth[1]; and typically hands on more acreage than he himself
inherited. (The average size of a full-time holding has increased
by about 20 per cent in the past decade.) Are there, however,
any valid arguments based on what a standard treatment for
CTT might imply for the efficiency and growth of farming to
sustain the case of the farming lobby that the current review
of CTT should continue, and indeed greatly increase, the special
treatment of farmers?

The following arguments have been frequently advanced.

(i) Farms as small businesses
CTT gives relief to the assets of all small businesses; and UK
agriculture is a collection of small businesses. Without relief,
there would be a threat to the survival of existing farmers; and
a deterrent to the entry of fresh blood.

The average full-time farm in the sample analysed for the
Farm Management Survey (Annual) in 1977 had about 230 acres
(93 hectares); regularly employed 1.8 workers in addition to
the farmer and his wife; had a turn-over of £40,000, and
required £38,000 of assets other than land and buildings; so
for this range of indicators the 'average' full-time farmer is not
large. However, it would have been worth in 1977 about
£210,000, net of liabilities, which averaged only 10 per cent
of net worth; and there is a considerable upper tail of very
much greater sizes of farm - see table 5.3 below. So 'smallness'
is not a universal characteristic.

More fundamentally, the case for tax relief for farmers could not be the same as that for 'small businesses' in general. With a fixed amount of land, and an increase in average size, the number of farms must inevitably decline. Employment will not be generated, but will continue to fall as productivity rises. Farms are not new enterprises - inheritance is practically the only method of entry, for tenant or owner. Finally, farms do not enjoy economies of scale as they get larger - see below. Hence the gains in efficiency, enterprise, employment and dynamic growth which form the case for interfering with equity and so for reducing CTT on the assets of unincorporated businesses in general are not at all characteristic of farming.

(ii) The allegedly low yield in farming
It is frequently claimed that the price at which agricultural land would be valued for CTT, if there were no reliefs, would 'greatly exceed its agricultural value'. Consequently it is claimed that the purely agricultural return to the farmer would not be great enough to pay CTT, because 'the yield is only 2 per cent or 3 per cent'. Therefore, it is alleged, land would certainly have to be sold.

Which outsiders are supposed to be driving the price of land up in this way? Institutions which are tax exempted (Pension Funds) or tax favoured (Insurance Companies), or foreigners, were said to be to blame. However, the evidence given to Northfield (para. 330) was that institutions bought 5½ per cent of the vacant possession land sold in 1976, and 6 per cent in 1977; and foreigners bought very much less than that. Farmers themselves are the main buyers. The price they pay reflects their informed expectations about likely future agriculture incomes - plus two factors not usually mentioned. The first of these is the capital gain that is likely to accrue (since 1969 the gain has been about £1,000 per acre - or about a quarter of a million pounds on the average farm). The second is the capitalisation into the value of the land of the existing, and hoped for, tax concessions - which include Capital Gains Tax roll-over relief, as well as the CTT reductions mentioned below.

The increase in agricultural incomes is normally obscured by the emphasis given by both MAFF and the NFU to the estimates published each year in the Annual Review of Agriculture of what is described as 'aggregate net income excluding stock appreciation'. This number relates also to part-time farmers (who outnumber the 125,000 full-time ones); assumes (until 1979) that all farmers pay rent, although 60 per cent of them do not; and excludes every year the value of the increase in growing crops and in livestock.

A better though still imperfect guide to the trend in income of the full-time farmers of different types and sizes is provided by the Farm Management Survey data (Annual). Using this to calculate income per acre for the average farm, net of depreciation but including appreciation on stock and work in

progress, deflated each year by the Retail Price Index, but not
adding back either imputed rent or the effect of the increase
in farm size since 1969, gives the following series for net income
per acre in 1969 prices:
Year: 1969 1970 1971 1972 1973 1974 1975 1976 1977
Income per acre: 12.9 14.0 20.8 26.5 27.7 20.5 26.0 24.4 20.7

As can be seen, real incomes per acre on this basis more than
doubled between 1969 and 1973 (with increases of 48 per cent
in 1970-1, and 27 per cent in 1971-2), and then fell back somewhat. (For the years after 1977-8 the published data on net income by size of farm are unfortunately collected on a different
and incompatible set of definitions.) Plainly, any calculation of a
growth rate derived from a comparison of just an initial and
terminal year, and so ignoring the experience of these intermediate years, will be very misleading.

Further, when it is said 'the yield on agricultural land is
exceptionally low' the definition of 'yield' is simply first-year
income divided by first-year capital value. Fallacious arguments
about the alleged 'low yield' and 'high capitalisation' in farming
are frequently used to reach erroneous conclusions about the
difficulty of entering farming; and about the 'low income' of
farmers. Thus, to quote some recent instances:
(a) The Agricultural EDC (1978), in 'The Impact of Taxation',
at 3.7, put it thus: 'Agricultural land, the yield from which is
abnormally low compared with that on capital assets in other
businesses and therefore less adequate to meet the funding costs
of any capital tax liability...'
(b) The Northfield Committee (para. 203) put it thus: 'the
return on capital - and particularly that proportion of the
capital which is represented by land - is low'.
(c) A study (1979) from Manchester University Department of
Agricultural Economics says that because 'the cost of starting
up in farming has increased by 50 per cent in one year' there
must be compensatory increases in income for the new entrants
if dire, though unspecified, consequences are to be avoided.
(It is not explained how the enhanced incomes would be confined
only to new entrants. Perhaps that is why the fallacy is so
popular with farmers?)

The point is that farm land, unlike machines and most of the
other 'capital assets of businesses', is not reproducible. An
increase in its price therefore does not reflect an increase in
unavoidable production costs. Rather the price reflects what
the market is prepared to pay for the present value of expected
post-tax income stream that can be earned by owners of this
scarce asset, as modified by the expected tax advantages
enjoyed by farmers. So the hypothetical new farmer decides
to pay the current price for land only because he expects that
the post-tax return, in all of the relevant dimensions, will
be worth it - and greater than he could obtain elsewhere. That
'return' in real terms can be expressed either as a yield to
redemption (where the new entrant's expected capital gain on

the land is automatically included); or as a discounted cash
flow (DCF) return; or as the internal rate of return. What it
cannot be properly expressed as is the form adopted in all the
instances quoted here, viz., 'income in the first year as a
percentage of land price in the first year.' That bit of arithmetic may say something about liquidity – but not about rates
of return, since it leaves out income in years other than the
first, the terminal value of the land, and the tax advantages.

Thus, if the 'real net advantages stream' is thought to have
increased, then the internal rate of return (and the redemption
yield, and the DCF return) will rise, if land prices do not
rise. The increase in land prices following the expected increase
in the stream of net advantages is precisely what keeps the
yield on farm land in line with that on alternatives. The 'first
year return' naturally falls when the increase in yield is
prevented – because the change in land price (crudely, the
present value of many years' worth of increased income) is
greater than the change in only the first year's income. But
at the higher land price, the redemption yield is unchanged.

It is precisely because the market already believes that the
presently expected incomes likely to be earned by the next
generation of farmers will be much higher than those of their
fathers that land prices have risen. Contrary to the claims
made above, it is emphatically not the case that current income
prospects will have to be further improved if the new entrants
are to be kept in farming, or if existing ones are to have the
cash to pay taxes. The current prospects were quite good
enough to get them in – despite the low cash flow in the early
years for anyone who has to borrow heavily to enter the
club. And the alleged 'low yield' is not tempting many existing
farmers to sell out at the 'high price' for land in order to
invest in gilts or equities – precisely because they are well
aware of the agricultural reasons for the price. Further measures to increase incomes would simply raise land prices yet
further – and reduce 'first year return' further – as would
granting the further tax advantages so persistently pursued
by the farm lobby.

A fall in the first year return ('an increase in the cost of
starting in farming' or 'a decrease in the first year return on
capital') has happened because farmers are more prosperous,
not because their economic prospects have been diminished.

An estimate of the appropriate concept, which is the redemption yield in agriculture, can be made as follows. If the above
series for real income per acre at 1969 prices is augmented by
a capital input of £206 at the end of 1968 and the terminal
capital value of £412 in 1979, also at 1969 prices, and if a guess
is made for real incomes on a comparable basis in 1978-9, then
a combined real yield of income and capital gain of no less than
about 16 per cent emerges, over this period. The calculation is
rough; and the experience of the 1970s may not be repeated
– for instance, the UK can only enter the CAP once; but a real

yield of something like this order of magnitude is a more
accurate estimate of 'the agricultural yield' than the irrelevant
numbers for the first-year return which are often relied upon
to indicate an alleged inability to pay CTT.

Moreover, this calculation perforce makes the assumption that
all of the farmer's income is accurately recorded in the Farm
Management Survey. The Central Statistical Office reported
('Economic Trends', 1980, p. 85) some official estimates for tax
evasion. The self-employed are thought by the CSO to have
understated their collective incomes by 26 per cent in 1978.
Whether farmers exceed or fall short of this average degree of
evasion for the self-employed sector as a whole is not known.
But farmers may be presumed to know accurately what their
actual - and even their prospective - incomes are when they
decide how much to pay for more land.

Thus there are good grounds for arguing that the generally
impressive performance of agricultural land prices over the past
decade accurately reflects the expectations of the farmers who
are the main purchasers, and who are well informed about the
real agricultural return - income plus capital gain - that can
be expected from farming. Naturally as their CTT base increases,
farmers should expect their eventual CTT bill to rise also; but
the value of their assets rises just because their actual and
expected farming prospects have improved. It is not persuasive
for farmers to argue that as they get richer their taxes should
get smaller; but that is precisely what the 'low yield' and 'high
capitalisation' arguments amount to.

(iii) The farm fragmentation argument
A further line of argument that is often heard is that accrued
capital gain, however large, is not cash in hand; and some CTT
is likely to be payable in spite of the current reliefs. The cash
to pay tax (or to insure against it, see the section 'Insurance
against CTT' below) must therefore be either at the expense of
new investment; or require a sale of land; or - possibilities not
so frequently mentioned - a sale to a financial institution coupled
with a leaseback plus a tenancy to the heir; or a reduction in
the farmer's or his heirs' standard of living; or inability to
make further land acquisitions on the scale that he had done
so far; or the sale of non-agricultural assets - Inland Revenue
data show that the investment income of the larger farmers is
a significant proportion of their total income. It is then claimed
that this 'fragmentation', if it happens, would be a serious
threat to agricultural efficiency and would raise costs of production - and so tax relief should be big enough to ensure that
this fragmentation does not happen. It is worth noticing that,
even if this argument were valid, the workings of the CAP are
such that farmers not consumers tend to benefit from increases
in efficiency, and vice versa. Hence any efficiency loss in UK
farming would not automatically raise prices to the detriment
of UK consumers.

The main purpose of the following sections is to explore
further the questions: (1) How big does a farm have to be to
produce efficiently i.e. up to what size will there be economies
of scale? (2) How big is the CTT bill likely to be for farms of
this size? That involves the calculation of effective rather than
nominal tax rates by value of agricultural assets, allowing for
a range of tax planning. And then the calculation of land areas
appropriate to those total values. (3) How serious is the possibility that land will have to be sold to meet CTT? That is,
how difficult is it likely to be for farms up to the minimum efficient scale size to provide for CTT - either by taking out
insurance policies - or by paying the tax by instalments out of
income?

ECONOMIES OF SCALE IN FARMING

The earliest authoritative and quantitative analysis of the
economies of scale in UK farming appears to be that published
by the Natural Resources (Technical) Committee chaired by
Sir Solly Zuckerman (1961). The data related to conditions
mainly in 1952-6. That Committee studied how the inverse of
long-run unit cost, namely the average gross output per
hundred pounds of total input, varied by size and type of
farm. The diagram containing the major findings showed little
gain in efficiency beyond sizes of 200-300 acres. As the Committee put it, 'the rate of increase is greater in the smaller than
in the larger size ranges for all types of farm, and it is also in
the size groups below 100 acres that the difference in the
ratio between types of farms is greatest.'

The relief from CTT for agricultural land farmed by working
farmers was announced in November 1974 - and was at that
stage limited to 1,000 acres, a size exceeded by less than 1 per
cent of farmers. At that date there had apparently been *no*
further major official study of the relationship between size and
efficiency, since the Zuckerman Committee reported. However,
the official basic data collected in the Farm Management Survey
sample had become more refined.

The book by D.K. Britton and B. Hill (1975) was based on
the FMS data for 1970-1. Their analysis is based firmly on the
analysis of total factor productivity, that is, the output per
total input, which is the inverse of long-run unit average cost.
Thus they are not confined, as some other misleading studies
have been, to partial productivity indicators like yield per
acre, or profit on capital. They are also careful to distinguish
between the effect of spreading fixed costs over greater output,
which is a short-run phenomenon; and the effect on unit costs
of output when all of the factor inputs vary - which is the long-
run phenomenon known as economies of scale, if outputs do, in
fact, increase faster than total inputs, so that unit costs decline
with size. They summarised their 1975 results in 1978 thus:

Our principal finding on size and efficiency using data
drawn from the Farm Management Survey was that farms
of less than about 110-150 acres were generally less efficient than farms above that size.... Using data for 1970-1
we found that, when examining a cross-section of farms,
efficiency increased with farm size (area) sharply at first
but then at a decreasing rate, reaching a level beyond
which little, if any, further increases in efficiency were
observed. The acreage beyond which [statistically] significant improvements in efficiency did not appear to occur
was 100-150 acres for dairy farms, 150-200 acres for mixed
farms, 200-250 acres for cropping farms and 250-300 acres
for livestock (cattle and/or sheep-rearing farms).

In this paper, Britton and Hill (1978) then go on to report
the results of analysing data from the FMS for the six successive years 1968-73. They say:

The familiar pattern of improving performance as one proceeds up the size spectrum from the smallest to the medium-
sized farms is common to each farming type. The figures
generally confirm the indications based on only one year's
data, namely that (i) efficiency was significantly lower for
farms of below 100 acres than for farms in any of the
higher size groups; and (ii) beyond 400 acres there was
no consistent upward movement at the large end of the size
spectrum.

They examined also the efficiency of the very largest farms –
those of over 4,200 smd. (Size is here measured in terms of
'standard man days' of labour input. The corresponding size
in acres varies with the type of farming enterprise – but on
average is over 1,000 acres for this group of farms.) They
say:

our conclusions on the relative efficiency of the very large
farm is that there are *no grounds to support the argument
that these farms are on average more efficient than* medium-
sized farms. Indeed, among Cropping and Mixed farms there
is evidence that the largest performed noticeably less well
than some smaller size groups. Whatever other support the
protagonists for the protection of the large farm against the
impact of taxation may justifiably summon, it would be misleading on the evidence available to predict a widespread
fall-off in the general efficiency of the British agricultural
industry as a direct result of a reduction in numbers of the
very large farms, even of their total disappearance.... it
seems unlikely that the share of output generated by the
productive resources contained on these farms would fall
(and might even rise) if they were employed in somewhat
smaller businesses. (pp. 29-30)

The pioneering work of Britton and Hill has now been more
widely imitated - with the same general results. See, for
example, the work of two economists at MAFF and the studies
they cite - P.J. Lund and P.G. Hill (1979). They too speak
of 'a continuing increase through to about the 1800 smd size' -
which corresponds to an area of about 250-350 acres.

All of these conclusions relate to the average performance in
each of the size categories. The data show a wide dispersion in
efficiency at each size so that, for instance, some of the
smallest farms are more efficient than some of the largest farms.
However, the variance is approximately the same at each size,
so the relationship based on averages is not a distorted one.
Hence it is quite appropriate that fiscal policy, and claims for
exemption from its workings, should continue to be expressed
in terms of average performance at each size.

In the light of the evidence it is then clear that a fiscal regi-
men which forced farms to be split up into units as small as
100 acres would probably have an efficiency cost. If units which
had been larger than 250-300 acres were pushed into the size
region of 100-300 acres, then there might conceivably be some
efficiency cost. However, if units above 250-300 acres got
smaller but remained above 250-300 acres then some efficiency
gain is not impossible.

The potential burden of CTT on farms of different sizes is
calculated next as a background guide to the likelihood of
'fragmentation' when viewed against this set of benchmarks.
Note, however, that if one farm gets smaller the most typical
concomitant effect is that another farmer buys the land - and
so his farm becomes bigger. The 'fragment' is not typically
farmed as an independent (and inefficient) unit. That, indeed,
is the process known to lie behind the steady increase in average farm size. Farms already large when inherited get larger
during the lifetime of the successor, by acquisition. Hence
even if some farms were to be pushed below 300 acres by a CTT
sale, other farms would simultaneously rise above that size;
hence the average size of holding (and so average overall
efficiency) need not fall. Again, there is some evidence that
larger farms are very often 'fragmented' already, i.e., the
bigger the holding is the more likely is it that it is not made
up of contiguous fields; its total acreage may be widely scattered
geographically. Sale of the outlying acres would make the holding smaller but not more fragmented - and quite possibly less
so than it is already (see Edwards, 1978).

NOMINAL AND EFFECTIVE RATES OF TAX

To calculate the potential CTT charge on farms of differing
sizes it is necessary first to calculate tax liability at different
asset values; and then to interpret those results in terms of
physical size. The threshold was revised from £25,000 to

£50,000 in the March 1980 budget. The calculations here are
for March 1980. The major reductions of March 1981 are illustrated in a later section dealing with that budget and tables
5.6–5.8; and Sutherland (1981).

TABLE 5.1 *Effective tax rates on assets 1980*

Assets (£000)	A	B	C	D	E	F	G	H
50	0	0						
70	9	0	0					
110	21	3	1	½	0			
200	37	19	9	4	0	0	0	
300	45	30	15	7	6	3	3	0
510	51	42	21	10	13	6	6	3
700	55	47	23	12	17	8	7	4
1,010	58	51	25	15	21	10	9	6
2,010	64	58	29	18	25	15	12	9
3,000	68	62	31	20	28	17	14	10
4,000	69	64	32	21	29	18	15	12
10,000	73	71	35	23	33	22	19	17
30,000	74	73	37	25	36	24	20	19

Notes: A is the standard tax rate; and B is the rate if assets are split with a spouse; C is the
rate for a farmer, assuming only 50 per cent relief; D is the farmer's rate, allowing for
payment by interest-free instalments; E is the farmer's rate, after splitting with a spouse;
F is the farmer's rate, after splitting, and after allowing for instalments; G is the farmer's
rate, if the 'double discount' is enjoyed and if payment is by instalments, with interest;
H is the farmer's rate, if assets are split and the double discount applies, and if payment
is by instalments, with interest.

In Table 5.1 the first step is to calculate from the successive
marginal rates what the tax liability was in 1980 as a percentage
of the assets (the average tax rate) for a standard CTT payer
at death. As can be seen in column A, although a marginal
rate of 50 per cent is reached at assets of £100,000, the effective rate does not reach that level until half a million pounds.
One hopes that illustrative calculations of the effective rates
implied are provided to those taking the decisions, since the
implications of a schedule of marginal rates – which in all that
is typically presented by the Inland Revenue – elude easy
comprehension.

However, CTT is not payable on a transfer to a spouse. With
a progressive rate structure, splitting the assets into two
produces a smaller total tax bill, even without allowing for the
value of tax postponement on half the assets. Nor is it necessary
for the split to be made or agreed during life; a Deed of Family
Arrangement after the death of the first spouse can produce the
tax saving without any tax planning. (It should be noted that
Northfield is therefore quite wrong when it states (para. 208)

that 'there must be absolute trust between the partners' if the benefit of asset-splitting is to be obtained. The split can be accomplished by the survivor acting alone.) Hence, provided that there is a spouse, the relevant tax rate is that shown in column B, not that shown in A.

For working farmers, the principal modifications to column A are as follows.

1 Land up to 1,000 acres (per farmer i.e. 2,000 acres for husband and wife) is automatically entitled to the Agricultural Relief of 50 per cent, which was introduced with CTT itself in 1974. The effect is illustrated in column C. Above 1,000 acres each - say £2½ million in 1979 - Agricultural Relief is limited to 30 per cent. But Business Relief at 50 per cent usually takes over there anyway - see 2 below. With progressive rates, reducing the tax base by 50 per cent reduces the tax rate by more than half.

2 Business assets, including any land above 1,000 acres each, are now entitled to Business Relief at 50 per cent, without any upper asset limit. Business Relief, which is not, of course, confined to farming businesses, was not introduced until 1976, at 30 per cent. It was increased in 1977 to 50 per cent; the upper limit of £500,000 which had been promised in October 1977 was not in fact introduced in the April 1978 budget.

3 Splitting ownership with a spouse (before death or by Deed of Family Arrangement after it) produces column E. It is not known how many farmers do have a spouse, but since concern as usually expressed is for 'the family farm' it seems fair to regard column E as the starting point for considering the typical CTT burden, even if no further planning is done.

4 For all businesses, but not for the standard CTT payer, the tax bill on transfer at death is payable by instalments over eight years. Since November 1974 no interest is payable to the Inland Revenue in respect of the tax due on the first quarter of a million of business property - which is calculated after deducting the 50 per cent working farmer or business relief. That is, the instalment method is interest-free for the tax due on the payment by instalments on the first £½m worth of business assets belonging to each owner. On larger asset totals interest *is* charged at 6 per cent (on death) or 9 per cent (on a lifetime transfer). (Before 1981 the benefit of the interest-free provision was not obtainable when the double discount system described at 5 below had been enjoyed; but even when (rather low) interest has to be paid, the instalment system represents a discount of around one third.)

The tax liability is determined at the outset, and does not rise if the land continues to appreciate in value over the eight year period. Even if prices remain constant, so that there is no benefit to the taxpayer from paying in a depreciating currency, the automatic facility to make payment by instalments is a major concession. Thus compare the payment of £800 now, with payment of £100 per year for eight years. At a 10 per cent rate of

discount the present value of £100 a year for eight years is
£533 (and not £800). Thus the concession amounts to taking
one-third off the tax bill. If there is inflation at 15 per cent a
year, then payment by instalments is equivalent to taking 60
per cent off the bill; if inflation is 10 per cent, the present
value of the tax bill in current prices is more than halved.

If we assume inflation at 10 per cent, and a 10 per cent real
discount rate, then to allow properly for this substantial concession the average tax rates shown in columns C and E have
to be reduced (allowing for the ceiling above of a quarter of a
million each) to those shown in columns D and F. That is, the
effective rate, even at one million pounds is not 21 per cent
but rather 10 per cent. That should be compared with Northfield's assertion 'the proportion of an owner-occupier's [farm-
ing] wealth eroded by CTT liabilities is in any case unlikely
to exceed *about 35 per cent* of total assets even if no tax
planning is undertaken' (para. 215, my italics). Neither splitting with a spouse, nor payment by interest-free instalments
requires any tax planning. The true effective maximum for the
family farm is thus about 24 per cent – at asset values of
£30 million – see columns D and F.
5 A further very important method for reducing the tax bill by
reducing the tax base may be open to farmers able and willing
to take appropriate tax planning steps. Institutional constraints
on rents, plus the right of a tenant since 1976 to hand on his
tenancy to two eligible successors (plus the capitalised tax
relief incorporated in the price of owner-occupied land) mean
that tenanted land sells at a substantial discount on the vacant
possession price, e.g. 60 typically as compared to 100. If a
suitably constructed partnership exists, or is set up, then a
farm owned freehold by father, and valued at the vacant possession price, can become a jointly tenanted farm – with mother,
son (and one other partner) and father himself each having an
agricultural tenancy. Thus father still owns the freehold as well
as being one of the joint tenants. Although the tenancies create
no effective differences – the family farm is still owned, controlled and farmed by the family – the land on any transfer is
now valued for tax purposes at the tenanted price, not at the
owner-occupied price.

After this arrangement full Agricultural Relief is still obtainable at 50 per cent – on the much lower tenanted value of the
land. Since both the 50 per cent Agricultural Relief (designed
to protect the working farmer from the high price of vacant
possession land) and the tenanted value discount, can be
obtained, this method has become known as the double discount.
What then is the effect on a tax bill of setting up (or continuing) appropriate partnership/tenancy arrangements? As in
column G of Table 5.1, the tax base is reduced from 100 to 60 to
show the effects of obtaining tenanted valuation rather than
vacant possession value. The Agricultural Relief at 50 per cent
further reduces the tax base to 30. The effect on the average

tax rate is dramatic. (Above 1,000 acres per owner only 30 per cent Business Relief not 50 per cent will be obtained in many of these cases; that is allowed for in the table.)
6 Further, if the farmer splits ownership with a spouse, then both shares will be valued subject to the surviving tenancy. Thus the tax base of 30 is reduced further to two amounts of 15 - and column H shows the average tax rate on the sum of the two halves.

A suitably drawn partnership need not necessarily be confined to children or other relatives - any heir can be brought in, provided that there are acceptable commercial reasons for his entry to the partnership. Where a spouse is not involved, tax cannot be saved by splitting assets as in column H, but the major portion of the tax saving would still be possible in appropriate cases i.e. column G of Table 5.1.

The number of farmers able and likely to take advantage of the double discount method is not precisely known. Partnerships existing before CTT and so not subject to some of the following caveats on setting up new ones may nevertheless not be properly drawn so as to produce the maximum saving; for example, there must be a formal agricultural tenancy. New arrangements made since 1974 must also be carefully drawn to incorporate formal agricultural tenancies, and to make a market rent payable. Further, there could conceivably be a charge to CTT on the fall in value of the assets on the creation of the partnership - but only if the purpose can be shown to have been tax reduction rather than commercial. Normal commercial transactions are not likely to be affected, and it is generally accepted by the Inland Revenue that a farmer getting on in years may have good commercial reasons for bringing especially his children into partnership. Plainly farmers need specialised advice in order to make sure that their arrangements are appropriate. However, though none of the agricultural bodies giving evidence to Northfield mentioned such arrangements, there is nothing new in the concepts involved, which could be applied under estate duty also. The considerable scope that there may already be for farmers to take advantage of the double discount may be set in perspective by the evidence that partnerships account for about half of non-corporate farm profits.
7 Only the most obvious and well-known tax planning methods have been suggested here. Practitioners will be familiar with many more, for example the use of a change in the trustees of a self-administered pension fund to transfer control.

Tax liabilities have been calculated here for owner-occupiers. For tenants' assets - and typically an owner-occupier will also be partially a tenant also - the position between 1977 and 1981 is that they qualify for 50 per cent Business Relief; and can be split with a spouse; and tax can then be paid by instalments without interest. Hence columns D and F in Table 5.1 apply.

Until 1981 agricultural landlords paid CTT at the standard rate; so columns A and B applied. In addition, tax could be

paid by instalments, but with interest. Those landlords with
some land in hand (the large majority) do enjoy working farmer
relief for that part of their assets. The Agricultural EDC (1977)
calculated, on assumptions and with data which tend to increase
the estimate - for there is no comprehensive enumeration of
landlords by size of holding and the effect of payment by
instalments was ignored - that in 1977 landlords collectively
faced a CTT bill at an average rate of 49 per cent. A sale of
some tenanted land was thus likely to be forced on a landlord's
heir. However, if a let farm changes either occupiers or owners
it continues to produce food; and the evidence to Northfield
is that there is no significant change in farming efficiency or
output if either the freehold of previously let land is acquired
by the existing tenant; or if the landlord is able to farm himself; or if an existing owner-occupier buys the freehold of
additional land previously tenanted; or if an insurance company
or pension fund replaces a private landlord as owner - with
no change in the occupier, since the tenancy is protected. Thus
any case that there may be in terms of possible efficiency losses
from change in size of holding does *not* apply to change in the
ownership of holdings.

TAX RATE BY SIZE OF FARM

Plainly the size corresponding to a given asset value depends
on further assumptions about 'the' price of land at each date.
The upper quartile price is typically 50 per cent above the
mean - and the lower quartile 50 per cent below. So the resulting 'average' price has to be interpreted accordingly - but
bearing in mind that the income (and the capital gain) derived
from the best quality land will also be well above average.
(The net income of the farmer at the upper quartile for efficiency is typically five times higher than that of the farmer
at the lower quartile - see the FMS data.)
   Table 5.2 below gives index numbers of prices (with 1969 =
100) for vacant possession land, for ordinary shares, and for
retail prices. The final row shows real land price movements.
   In Table 5.4 below the asset value (and so the tax liability)
of each farm size has been calculated simply by multiplying
acres by the estimated average price of land as given in Table
5.2. Overall this method considerably exaggerates the tax,
on average, payable at a given acreage size, because:
(a) Liabilities (of typically 10 per cent) should be deducted
from assets.
(b) Many CTT events will consist of whole farms - and the
price per acre for instance above 297 acres (90 hectares) is
about 20 per cent below the mean for blocks of land of all sizes.
(c) Many CTT events will leave one joint owner as survivor -
and land valued subject to the interest of the survivor will be
10-20 per cent below full price.

TABLE 5.2 *Prices (1969 = 100)*

	1971	1972	1973	1974	1975	1976	1977	1978	1979	1980	Jan. 1981
Land[a]	113	222	303	247	229	277	381	485	614	604	583
Shares[b]	92	120	104	60	74	64	108	114	113	111	109
Retail Prices[c]	116	125	136	158	196	228	265	287	325	383	403
Land Price deflated by Retail Price	98	179	221	156	117	121	144	169	189	158	145

Notes: a. The price for sales with vacant possession of land and buildings is estimated from the comprehensive Inland Revenue data for England and Wales. The effect of a 9 month reporting lag has been removed — which means that the most recent annual data available relate to 1979; and then the series has been incremented at the rate of change revealed by the more up to date, but less comprehensive and typically higher, auction data published by the Agricultural Development Advisory Service. Thus the figure for the average price in 1980 (£1245), and for the point estimate at January 1981 (£1203) are both rather rough. Prices stopped rising sharply by the end of 1980, peaked in mid 1980, fell, and then were showing signs of recovery at the beginning of 1981. b. Shares is the FT (Ordinary) Index. c. Retail Prices is the RPI.

(d) The acres below are owned acres; but the 'average' farmer farms (and derives income from) rented land as well as his own land - and on a greater scale the larger his size. Thus up to 125 acres, 78 per cent of the land is his own; at 700-999 acres only 66 per cent is. Hence the typical 'mixed tenure' farmer operating on 125 acres has a tax liability corresponding to that shown here for 97.5 acres of owned land; and on 850 acres of land farmed the tax liability is that shown for 560 acres of land owned.

(e) Going the other way, farm assets other than the land and buildings (say 20 per cent) should be added to the tax base.

Taken together, the factors (a)-(d) which tend to amount to an over-statement of the land value, amount to approximately 50-70 per cent. (That is assuming that where the joint owner-ship factor is operating, then the size of holding factor does not operate at all.) Facter (e) goes the other way and requires 20 per cent to be added back. So the assets corresponding to a given size of farm are over-stated by a factor of between two and three. Hence, if the land price used in the following table puts a farm into the 300-acre size group, then in practice it might take a typical mixed tenure farm as big as 500-830 acres to generate the asset base that is used here. Alternatively, those who might for some particular reason regard land prices much higher than those used here as relevant at each date, because they are concerned with high quality farms only, could say that the effective tax rates on 300 acres would be reached on the average farm of that size - but only if land prices at each date were taken to be 40-56 per cent higher than those assumed here.

In order to put the data in perspective, Table 5.3 shows how

many farms there are in each size bracket and what percentage
of the acreage each size accounts for.

TABLE 5.3 *Number of farms in England and Wales by size*

acres	below 50	50-99	100-149	150-299	300-499	500-699	700-999	1,000+
(hectares, approx.)	below 20	20-40	40-60	60-121	121-202	202-282	282-401	401+
Number of holdings (rounded)	92,300	40,800	23,500	28,700	10,600	3,560	2,031	1,497
Percentage of acreage	7.5	12.5	12.1	25.3	17.1	8.8	7.1	9.6

Source: Agricultural Census, 1975.

Table 5.4 shows the effective rates of tax for farms of a given
acreage size over time. For 1974-9 the assumption is that the
1978 CTT Tax Schedules - somewhat higher than those shown
in Table 5.1 - and reliefs applied throughout. Because business
assets other than land and buildings have for simplicity been
ignored here (see above), the effect of the increasingly favourable treatment of such assets is perforce ignored. Thus for an
asset base including tenant's type assets the increase in effective tax rates over 1974-80 shown here is slightly exaggerated
by this omission. The 1980 column incorporates the effect of
raising the threshold for CTT from £25,000 to £50,000.

TABLE 5.4 *Tax rates by size of farm 1974-80 and capital gain and asset value 1980*

Acres		1974	1975	1976	1977	1978	1979	1980	Asset Value 1980 (£000)	Capital Gain 1975-80 (£000)
300	E	2	2	3	6	10	11	9	373	232
	F	1	1	1	3	5	5	4		
	H	0	0	0	1	2	2	1		
500	E	7	6	10	12	16	17	15	622	387
	F	3	3	5	6	8	8	7		
	H	1	1	1	3	4	5	3		
1,000	E	14	14	16	19	23	23	23	1,245	774
	F	7	7	8	9	11	12	11		
	H	3	3	4	5	7	8	7		

Notes: E is 50 per cent plus splitting; F is 50 per cent plus splitting plus the effect of
instalments; H is 50 per cent plus splitting plus double discount plus instalments with
interest.

The effective rates are calculated for three of the assumptions used in Table 5.1, that is 50 per cent relief plus asset splitting with a spouse (*E*); that plus instalments (*F*); those reliefs with in addition the double discount (*H*). The average size of a full-time holding (crops and grass) is about 240 acres.

For tenant's assets Table 5.5 shows the effect over the period 1974-6 of Business Relief, which was introduced at 30 per cent in 1976 and increased to 50 per cent in 1977. The tax rates for 1980 can be read off from Table 5.1 above in column *F*. The FMS data suggests that on the average size of farm the tenant's net assets would be about £57,000 in 1979, and so the average tax rate is zero. The £300,000 figure shown in Table 5.5 would not have been reached until well over 1,000 acres.

TABLE 5.5 *Tenants' assets: effective tax rates*

£000	1974-6			1976-7			1977-9		
	I	II	III	I	II	III	I	II	III
30	2	–		–	–		–	–	
50	10	0.4	–	2	–		–	–	
70	16	4	2	4	–		2		
110	26	12	6	9	3	–	6	0	–
200	39	24	12	22	11	5	12	5	2
300	46	32	15	28	17	8	16	9	4

Notes: I if no splitting; II assets split with a spouse; III plus interest-free instalments.

INSURANCE AGAINST CTT

There is one further major step to be considered. That is the use of insurance policies to provide now from farming or other income sources for those CTT liabilities that are expected to arise in future. This method does not reduce the tax liability, unlike the methods considered previously, but it does provide a way of avoiding the risk of having to sell any assets - farm assets or other types of assets. Suitable insurance policies would be written in trust for the heirs so that the proceeds would incur no CTT in the hands of the recipients, and so could be used in their entirety to pay the CTT on the inheritance.

How much insurance cover will be required? Could the premium be met out of income? The answers to these questions depend, among other things, on the likely tax liability - which depends on which of the tax reduction methods available the farmer is able to take, as well as on the market value of his assets. The answers also depend on the farmer's objectives, and in particular on how much of his own current income he is prepared to forgo in order to hand on his farm, with its increasing earn-

ing power, intact. If the farmer does intend to try to hand on
to his heirs the whole of the farm, at the size to which it has
grown over his lifetime, then he should, of course, insure for
the full amount of the prospective CTT liability - and plan to
increase it in later years. An accurate assessment of the future
liability would require a forecast of both future asset prices;
and of future tax schedules, and tax exemptions. These tasks
are not attempted here.

An average quotation for a low-cost whole life policy for a
man aged 44 (that is, a with profits policy combined with
decreasing term assurance cover) would give cover of about
£147,000 for a gross premium of £2,000 (that is, a net premium
of £1,650, assuming tax relief for the full amount). It will be
remembered that until 1981 £2,000 is the maximum standard
annual exemption per person for a gift, if CTT is to be avoided
on it.

The average full-time farm (of 229 acres, mixed tenure) in
1977 would have had an insurance cost of between 41 pence per
acre on assumption E in Table 5.1; and nil on assumption H.
The income per acre for a farm of average efficiency, and adding back 80 per cent of the imputed rent, was about £55, according to the FMS; and about £133 per acre for a farm at the top
decile for efficiency.

For the 500 acre farm the insurance cost would have been
£1.24 per acre on assumption E; and 20 pence on assumption
H.

By September 1979 land prices had risen substantially;
insurance costs per acre would then be between £1.80 and 24
pence on 229 acres; and between £3.40 and 67 pence on 500
acres. 1979 incomes are not known. Each of the insurance costs
quoted should be reduced substantially to allow for the effect
of mixed tenure in reducing the tax base (see p. 106 (d)).

Especially for a farmer whose farm is no more than twice the
average size and is prepared and able to arrange his affairs so
as to reduce his prospective CTT bill, it does not appear to
involve great expense, even at the rates current in 1979, in
order to insure for the *whole* of the CTT liability and so to
protect his heirs from any attrition whatever of the physical
farm. If land prices rise in future then more insurance will be
needed; but then more income will be available also.

INFLATION EFFECT

What is the position likely to be if inflation continues? Table
5.4 already shows how the rise in land prices between 1975 and
1979 had affected the tax rate, since it was constructed by
applying the 1979 CTT tax schedules to these earlier years.
Because the effective tax rate schedule was not very progressive
even then, it can be seen that an increase in land prices, by a
factor of 2.68 between 1975 and 1979, left most of the capital

gain to the heir. For instance, on assumption E, even on 500
owned acres the after-tax assets would have increased from
£221,000 to £524,000 - an increase by a factor of 2.37. The real
value of each acre had increased markedly, by a factor of about
1.6 between 1975 and 1979 - see Table 5.2 above; if that real
increase continues it will be that phenomenon and not any
sharply progressive tax schedule that will be the main factor
producing an increase in real CTT liability for farmers.

BEFORE THE 1981 BUDGET

Before the further reductions in CTT in 1981, my conclusion
Sutherland (1980) was:

> The capital transfer tax concessions to all farmers, regard-
> less of their size or efficiency, go well beyond what is
> required to preserve an efficient farm size structure, and
> are both inequitable, and an obstacle to new entrants to
> farming. However, partly because the long history of tax
> concessions has been capitalised into the existing price of
> land, and partly because there are genuine economies of
> scale up to about 250-300 acres, it would be unduly dis-
> ruptive to restore all farmers to full standard CTT liability.
> I would therefore support a reform which confined the full
> existing concession (which reduces the tax base to 50% of
> market value) to land up to 200 acres per family farm - not
> per individual family member; with a tapering of relief down
> to zero at 400 acres. I would also close the loophole which
> allows many family partnerships to apply the 50% valuation
> reduction not to the vacant possession value but to the
> much lower tenanted value.
>   Such a reform would have minimal effects on farm output
> and farm efficiency - indeed both might well improve; but
> it would move towards equity between tax payers; would
> reduce the government's borrowing requirement; and would
> encourage a move away from the hereditary closed shop that
> farming has become.

THE 1981 BUDGET AND THE DEMISE OF CAPITAL TRANSFER TAX

The 1981 budget has moved policy towards CTT in general, and
agriculture in particular, even further in a direction which has
no intellectual justification. The reductions in CTT relevant to
agriculture are:

A Concessions given to everybody, viz:
(a) instead of the lifetime cumulation of transfers, and one tax-
exempt tranche of £50,000, cumulation is now limited to ten

years; (b) the annual exemption is to be £3,000 instead of £2,000; (c) very much lower tax rates for lifetime transfers – see Table 5.6 below, which also shows the effective death rate.

TABLE 5.6 *Effective tax rates for lifetime and death transfers 1980 and 1981*

Taxable amount[a] £000	Lifetime transfers pre-budget	now	Death transfers[b] single	split with spouse
60	2	2	½	
70	5	5	9	0
90	8	7		
110	11	10	21	3
130	13	12		
160	17	16		
210	23	20	37	19
260	28	23		
310	33	25	45	30
510	43	29	51	42
1010	54	34	58	51
2010	62	40	64	58

Notes: a. For personally owned farms/businesses, the 50 per cent valuation reduction has to be deducted from the market value of the assets to arrive at the appropriate 'taxable amount' of column 1 here. E.g. farm assets of £1 million produce a taxable amount of half a million pounds, etc. b. In the case of transfers at death, the schedule of rates here assumes that there have been no tax-free tranches to deduct first. See p. 113, and Table 5.8, lines 1 and 2.

B Concessions for personal proprietors/partners of businesses, farms:
(d) any tax due can, as before, be paid by eight annual instalments, with the difference that the limit of a quarter of a million pounds, above which interest had to be paid, has now been abolished.

C Concessions for agricultural landlords:
(e) previously tax paid by instalments had to be accompanied by interest, with no quarter of a million pounds exemption. Now they too will have interest-free instalments, without any upper limit; (f) a new valuation relief, knocking 20 per cent off the value of tenanted land. (Farmers/businessmen already have a 50 per cent reduction.)

D Implications of the new concessions:
(a) plus (b) The standard payer of CTT can now transfer £80,000 every ten years (i.e. £50,000 plus £3,000 per year) tax-free; and a couple can transfer £160,000. Over any eleven year period these sums become £113,000 and £226,000. Anyone with assets of even £160,000 is in the *top 1 per cent* of wealth-owners.

The Financial Statement (p. 10) 'is unable to estimate' the cost of this concession. The revenue loss (never mind equity!) will be enormous, since in future almost no one will have to pay any CTT.

For farmers/businessmen the 50 per cent valuation relief has to be applied before calculating the tax-free amounts. Thus it is £160,000 per decade per person, and £320,000 for a couple (and £226,000 and £532,000[2] for any eleven-year period).

There are about 121,000 full-time farms; and the average size is now about 240 acres. Such a farm is currently worth (land, buildings, farm assets) about a third to half a million pounds. Thus family farms of average size or below can now pay zero CTT. Farms much above average size will also be able to avoid CTT entirely by using minimal foresight and so enjoying more than just the terminal tranche of tax-free transfers.

(c) Lifetime transfers. The Treasury 'Economic Progress Report' (like the Chancellor) continues to talk misleadingly about 'maximum rates' for lifetime transfers going down from 75 per cent to 50 per cent. But 50 per cent is the tax rate payable only on that portion which is above £2 million. The average (or effective) tax rate on £2 million was 62 per cent; and will now be 40 per cent; at £1 million it was 54 per cent; and now 34 per cent. Table 5.6 gives a full schedule of these rates.

Moreover, the £1 million and £2 million are amounts of tax base, i.e. for farm or business assets the rates quoted arise on amounts of double that, that is, for them the tax on £2 million is now 34 per cent.

The tax concessions for transfers at death ((a) above) are now so generous that only the extremely rich will need to take advantage of (c). Moreover, the concessions are *not* confined to business assets - and so are not to be justified by any arguments about the merits of facilitating the handing on of family businesses. The extremely rich will benefit considerably - and the benefit of £4 million per annum estimated in the Financial Statement will be shared by very few i.e. the amount per head will be large.

(d) Instalments, interest-free. For those who still have a CTT bill, despite the ten-year's tranches tax-free, the benefit from being allowed to pay by interest-free instalments over eight years is a reduction of over a half in the present value of the tax - calculated above on page 103. (The Financial Statement estimate of £5 million is unbelievably low; there is certainly no inclusion there of the cost to the Revenue of being paid in depreciating currency.)

The old ceiling for interest-free instalments of a quarter of a million pounds meant half a million after allowing for 50 per cent relief; and so £1 million per couple. So even then this concession alone halved the effective tax rate even for farms of around three times the average size. Abolishing the ceiling therefore benefits that sub-set of the 3,500 farms which are bigger than this i.e. 700 acres/283 hectares *and* for which their owners took no steps to part with ten years before death. Economies of scale in farming run out at less than half this size of farm (see above); so there is absolutely no agricultural case for extending this concession thus.

In addition to the very largest farms, the beneficiaries will include those smaller farmers who have already taken steps to exploit the double discount loophole, that is, those farmers who have formed a family partnership designed to get the 50 per cent vacant possession relief on the (much lower) tenanted value, see Table 5.1 above, columns *G* and *H*. Even the Chancellor now thinks this is too much – and so proposes to reduce the advantages in future – though only after they have been enjoyed once. But in the meantime the advantages have been considerably increased, since all of the existing properly formulated partnerships will now be able to pay by interest-free instalments too. (Over half of farm profits accrue to partnerships.)

Table 5.7 shows the effective tax rates, pre- and post-budget, corresponding to the various assumptions about the circumstances shown in the notes to the table. (The figures for landlords are discussed below.)

Low though those Table 5.7 rates are (and were already, for farmers), the ones shown apply to a taxable amount of half a million pounds, etc. The ending of lifetime cumulation means that the taxable amount at death relevant for someone who initially owns assets worth half a million pounds will depend on how much the owner has already transferred tax free (i.e. how many decades' worth of exemptions) and on how much he transfers at the much lower lifetime rates of tax shown in Table 5.6. Table 5.8 here allows for this by showing the tax rates corresponding to a transfer of assets that were worth half a million pounds, etc., before father started handing them on. The calculations are done on the minimalist assumptions that only one earlier decade's worth of free exemptions has been taken in addition to the final i.e. eleventh year exemption; and that no lifetime rate transfers have been made. The rates are therefore very conservatively estimated. (The richer the taxpayer, the greater the incentives to do better than is implied by these assumptions.) In Table 5.8 the pre-budget rates from Table 5.7 are repeated in the 'then' column; and the 'now' column shows the effect of the post-budget reliefs plus the above minimalist assumptions about how many times they are enjoyed.

The average farm is worth no more than, say, half a million pounds; so with a wife, the rate was less than 6 per cent; and is now zero (line labelled 11 in Table 5.8). At twice average size, worth £1 million, the married rate was 10 per cent; and now is 5 per cent. For double-discount partnerships it was 6 per cent at £1 million; and now is 3 per cent. The evidence is that all of the important economies of scale can be achieved by farms no bigger than average size; i.e. there is no agricul-

TABLE 5.7 *Effective rates of CTT 1980 and 1981 (percentages)*

See note: 1			Asset value		
			£½m	£1m	£10m
	Standard payer				
		single owner	51	58	73
2		split with wife	42	51	71
pre-budget	Landlord				
3		single	34	39	49
4		with wife	28	34	48
post-budget 5		single	18	22	28
6		with wife	14	19	27
	Farmer/Businessman				
pre-budget 7		single	10	15	23
8		with wife	6	10	22
9		and family partners	3	6	17
post-budget 10		single	10	11	16
11		with wife	6	10	15
12		and family partners	2	4	12

Notes: 1. The assets are those left over to be taxed at death after the tranches of tax-free amounts per decade have been deducted. 2. The effect of reduced progression when assets are split into halves and tax is then calculated on the two sums. 3. The effect of paying by instalments, even with interest. 4. As 2. 5. The effects of (a) 20 per cent valuation reduction plus (b) instalments at death are now interest-free. 6. As 2. 7. The effect of 50 per cent valuation reduction plus instalments interest free up to ceiling of £¼m, with interest above that. 8. As 2. 9. The additional effects of giving the 50% valuation reduction on the tenanted value of the land, plus instalments with interest. 10. and 11. The improvements (on large amounts only) follow from removing the £¼m ceiling for interest-free instalments. 12. The effect of allowing interest-free instalments on existing 'double discount' arrangements.

tural gain in encouraging the survival of farms larger than this. And one has to have very peculiar notions of equity to think that even for farms of average size the CTT rate should be zero (when it is 23 per cent – now itself too low – on a standard payer, typically a widow, handing on family assets also worth an initial half a million pounds).

(e) Landlords. Before the budget they could pay by instalments (as the standard payer cannot) but with interest. If the interest was always as much as the landlord's cost of capital – and it frequently is lower than this – then with an inflation rate still held at 10 per cent, the burden was reduced from £800 to £533, i.e. by one-third. (See page 102; and see Table 5.7 above for the effects.) Removing the interest charge decreases the burden further to £383, i.e. to less than half. (f) Allowing for the 20 per cent relief on value, the tax rate on let land worth £1 million (say 1,400 acres/570 hectares), owned jointly with a spouse, was 34 per cent; and now will be (Table 5.8) 14 per cent.

TABLE 5.8 *Effective rates of CTT 1980 and 1981 (percentages) with one decade's worth of tax-free transfer*

See note		Tax rate	Value of assets initially					
			£½m		£1m		£10m	
			Then	Now	Then	Now	Then	Now
	Standard payer							
1	single owner	51	42		58	53	73	72
2	split with wife	42	23		51	41	71	69
	Landlord							
5	single	34	14		39	19	49	27
6	with wife	28	6		34	14	47	26
	Farmer/businessman							
10	single	10	5		15	10	23	17
11	with wife	6	0		10	5	22	15
12	and family partners	3	0		6	3	17	11

See page 114 for the assumptions and methods. The numbers in column 1 refer to the explanatory notes in Table 5.7 above.

There are no regular official statistics for the number of agricultural landlords, nor for their sizes (nor, indeed, for the amounts of non-agricultural wealth that they own). The Agriculture EDC (1977) made a crude attempt, with a non-scientific 'sample' of 18 per cent of the let areas. Their 18 per cent sample had 1,677 estates in it (Table 4.3 there); and half of the let land was in the 153 estates of over 3,000 acres each. Thus the bulk of the let land is likely to be in estates whose value begins at over £2 million (with a current price of around £700 per acre). Not all of the 153 are owned personally; but around 100 probably were. Grossing up from the sample, this suggests that there were about 550 personal landlords worth more than £2 million each. They are the principal beneficiaries of the Chancellor's proposals here.

CONCLUSIONS

1 The way that CTT rates are published (showing the marginal rates only) means that the effective (average) rates of tax have to be cranked out privately – as is done in Tables 5.6 and 5.7 here. Moreover, the cumulative effect of reliefs on valuation,

interest-free instalments, tax-free amounts per decade, etc.
are impossible to see at all, unless mechanical calculation is
supplemented by assumptions about behaviour - as in Tables
5.7 and 5.8. Does even the Chancellor realise (a) how low the
effective rates were for working farmers? and (b) by how much he
has reduced the rates for agricultural landlords? (If he were to
think the reduction was 'only about 20 per cent in line with the
new valuation relief', then Table 5.8 shows he would be wrong.)
If he does realise the implications of what he has done, why
does he not take credit for the practical abolition of CTT?
2 Ending lifetime cumulation means that even those standard
payers who are at the margin for entering the top 1 per cent
of the wealth distribution will now be able to escape CTT
entirely.
3 The concessions removing the 'quarter of a million pounds'
ceiling (not reached until a family business is worth £1 million)
for interest-free instalments of tax due on personally owned
businesses and farms go further than the government's objectives of encouraging small businesses can possibly require.
There should be some ceiling.
4 Working farmers had such large reliefs already that the new
concessions benefit mainly farms of several times the average
size - which are well above the point beyond which there are
no further economies of scale in farming.
5 The withdrawal of the benefits of the double-discount system
of family partnerships does not take place until after the first
post-budget occasion on which they are enjoyed (which may be
in twenty years time.) In the meantime all the existing exploi-
ters of this loophole have had the advantages greatly increased.
6 The special concessions for agricultural landlords (20 per
cent relief plus interest-free instalments) have no special
agricultural justification, and were not recommended by the
Northfield Committee.
7 Such general arguments as there may be for striving to
encourage new small businesses in general do not apply to the
very different circumstances of farming.
8 The Chancellor's reductions in CTT in the 1981 budget will
mean that almost all personally owned businesses will have very
low tax rates e.g. even on assets worth as much as £4 million -
quite big enough to merit a Stock Exchange quotation - the
effective tax rate will be less than 12 per cent once in a generation, that is about 0.4 per cent a year. A charge as low as
this will mean that personal wealth remains distributed with
extreme inequality. The Chancellor has ensured that the heir
of a multi-millionaire will also be in that position, provided
that father takes steps to use his wealth to buy a partnership,
and a sleeping one will do, in a suitable business or farm.
Efficiency and entrepreneurship can be fostered without such
inequitable results.

NOTES

* A fuller and earlier version of this chapter was prepared
  by the author before he resigned as Special Adviser to the
  Northfield Committee; that is on deposit in the Ministry of
  Agriculture Library. Grateful acknowledgment is made to
  the Institute for Fiscal Studies for permission to incorporate
  material from articles first published by them in 'Fiscal
  Studies', March 1980 and November 1981.
  In 1979, only 0.6 per cent of the adult population owned
  marketable wealth in excess of £100,000 each. Inland
  Revenue Statistics, 1981, Table 4.8.
2 I.e. a further £50,000 exemption plus £3,000 annual is
  £53,000. Relief at 50 per cent produces £106,000 each: so
  in the first year of the new decade the couple has a further
  £212,000 to add to the £320,000.

Rates and the distribution of income: fact and fantasy

Anthony Christopher

CONS AND PROS

In a lecture delivered to the Commonwealth Conference of Heads
of Valuation Departments in September 1980 Mr Elmer Cronk
(Assessor for New Brunswick-Canada) pointed out that in the
early 1930s a critic of the property tax said:

> If any tax could have been eliminated by adverse criticism,
> the general property tax should have been eliminated long
> ago. One searches in vain for one of its friends to defend
> it intelligently. It is even difficult to find anyone who has
> given it careful study who can subsequently speak of its
> failure in temperate language. Should some prosecuting
> attorney drag the tax as a culprit before the bar of justice,
> he would be embarrassed by the abundance of expert evi-
> dence against it.

He went on to point out that nevertheless the tax persists and
'pretty obviously planning for the eradication of the property
tax is a great deal easier than the eradication itself' (Cronk,
1981, p. 12). What is the 'expert evidence against' rates?
The Report of the Committee of Inquiry into Local Government
Finance, chaired by Frank, now Sir Frank, Layfield QC, stated
in May 1976 that there were four main criticisms (Layfield,
1976), namely that:

1 rating is regressive, that is, it takes a bigger share of
the income of poorer households than richer ones;

2 rating assessments are arbitrary and unfair because assessments vary widely for what is apparently the same type of
house;

3 that the rates paid by individual households bear no relationship to their income;

4 there are extra earners in some households who enjoy local services, but do not pay local taxes.
There are, as well, complaints that:
5 rating is a tax on a necessity of life, and
6 the tax is not related to the benefit which people derive from local services.
John Heddle MP in his booklet 'The Great Rate Debate' (Heddle, 1980) mentions additionally:
7 householders consider they are shouldering a disproportionate share of the burden of paying for local services (industry considers that it is the group that is hard done by);
8 less than half of those who vote in local government elections pay rates, which means that 19 million people do not;
9 most people do not understand the basis of rating valuation;
10 rateable values based on infrequent valuations are out of date for most of the time and, because the present system is based on hypothetical rental evidence, considerable anomalies exist;
11 rates are inadequate as taxes to finance local government services;
12 rates are insufficiently elastic to respond to increases in price levels due to the fact that such increases affect the property values over a relatively long period of time.
Before examining some of these criticisms in detail it is only fair to point out that defenders of the system can point to several advantages of the local property tax. These are summarised in 'The Future Shape of Local Government Finance' (1971), thus:
1 the yield of rates is substantial, certain and predictable and straightforward increases in poundages secure proportionate increases in yield;
2 rates are a tax on fixed property which is unambiguously related to one particular area and cannot be transferred to another area to take advantage of a lower level of taxation;
3 the burden falls to a large extent on local electors and can be perceived. There is a direct link between the level of local services and what must be paid to finance them;
4 there is virtually no scope for evasion and local variations present no difficulty;
5 the cost of collection and administration, including the cost of valuation, is low by comparison with costs that would be entailed in local operation of other possible taxes.
To these points John Heddle would add:
6 the more valuable the property, the higher are the charges;
7 rates are the sole independent tax source available to local authorities;
8 rates enable the community to recoup some element of the value which it creates;
9 rates produced for 1980/81 a total of £8,500 million, with industry and commerce contributing £2,994 million thereof ('Hansard', 24.7.1980, col. 378);

10 it is an open system of taxation with every ratepayer able
to see any assessment and the breakdown of expenditure;
11 as tempered by the variety of reliefs, the system now has
the nature of a proportional system of taxation which places it
in a middle position between progressive and regressive taxes.

THE REGRESSIVE CHARACTER OF RATES

This matter was studied after the 1963 Revaluation by the Committee of Inquiry into the Impact of Rates on Households under
the Chairmanship of Professor R.C.D. Allen CBE (Allen, 1965)
and he pointed out (Table 200) that in the residential field,
in households with an income of under £312 p.a., rates as a
percentage of disposable income were 8.2 per cent and in the
£312-£520 group they were 6.2 per cent. However, in the
£1,040-£1,560 group they represented 2.7 per cent, and in the
top group of £1,560 and over, 2.2. per cent. The Committee
commented that those figures show clearly the regressive nature
of rates as a tax *taken in isolation* (my italics). In the same
table they give figures for income tax, surtax and national
insurance contribution which amount to £2.1 in the lowest band
and £375.7 in the highest. The result is that rates are about
nine times national taxes in the lowest band and national taxes
are nine times rates in the highest. Adding rates and national
taxes together the percentages are shown to be 9 per cent at
the lowest end compared with 17.9 per cent at the top end. The
significance of this is that rates in fact provide only a proportion of the cost of local services, the balance being made up
from Central Government Funds, thus the contributions made
by individuals to the cost of local services should not be gauged
solely by their rate contributions.

As a result of the report of the Allen Committee the rate
rebates scheme was introduced in 1966 and it was extended in
scope in April 1974. Recognising that circumstances had changed
materially between 1965 and the mid 1970s, the Layfield Committee commissioned the Social Survey Division of the Office
of Population Censuses and Surveys (OPCS) to re-interview
households who co-operated in the Family Expenditure Survey
in the second quarter of 1974. The re-interview obtained
details of income, household composition, accommodation, housing costs and rating information. In connection with the last,
data was obtained both as to the amount of rates demanded
(called 'Gross Payment') and the amount of rates paid by the
householder after taking account of rate rebates and supplementary benefits (called 'Net Rate Payment'). The figures for
net rates assume that those families eligible for rebates, etc.
take them up; although the Committee deduced that in fact
15 per cent of those eligible did not do so.

The conclusions of the summary are set out in Annex 19 of
the Layfield Report and show, in fact, various progressive

factors. Thus, firstly, rateable values are broadly progressive with gross household income per week as Table 6.1 shows.

TABLE 6.1 *Average rateable values of households by range of Gross Household Income (England and Wales, 1974)*

	Range of Gross Household Income (GHI) per week								
	to £20	to £30	to £40	to £50	to £60	to £70	to £80	over £80	All households
Percentage of all households	16	9	10	12	12	10	9	22	100
Average rateable value (£)	121	152	161	152	170	189	188	246	178

Source: Family Expenditure Survey, April-September 1974. Reproduced from Layfield (1976), Table 34.

Secondly, gross rates are steeply regressive as can be seen from line 3 of Table 6.2.

Thirdly, net rates, after allowing for rebates etc. are progressive as can be seen from line 4 of the same table where they vary from nil in households earning up to £20 per week to a maximum of £2.5 at £50 per week, and fall away again to £1.7 with households earning over £100 per week. Obviously these averages conceal a wide range of variations in individual cases. Fourthly, that when considering both rates and national taxation together (as had the Allen Committee), but now taking account of net rate payments in place of gross payments, the total average bill per household is progressive as can be seen from lines 7 and 7a of Table 6.3.

Summing up this aspect the Green Paper, 'Local government finance' (Cmnd 6813, 1977, p. 17, para. 6.6) reported that the Layfield Committee examined the criticisms and concluded that:

rates are in fact progressive for lower income earners, due largely to the assistance given to nearly one third of households by the rate rebate scheme and in supplementary benefit. Rate payments in relation to incomes have remained remarkably stable in recent years. Although earning non-householders do not pay rates directly, all who pay national taxes contribute indirectly to the large part of local spending met by Government grant. Rates are not wholly a tax on a necessity. The degree to which people spend their incomes on housing and accommodation varies widely, and for a proportion of ratepayers contains some element of personal choice. Moreover, to the extent that rates represent a tax on a minimum level of accommodation, the rate rebates scheme

TABLE 6.2 *Average rate payments by range of Gross Household Income (Great Britain April-May 1975)*

Average rate payments	Range of Gross Household Income (GHI) per week												All households
---	to £20	to £25	to £30	to £35	to £40	to £45	to £50	to £60	to £70	to £80	to £100	over £100	
Average rate payments													
1 Gross rates £ per week	1.15	1.37	1.58	1.49	1.46	1.51	1.58	1.48	1.56	1.76	1.84	2.27	1.6
2 Net rates £ per week	nil	0.13	0.29	0.56	0.92	1.02	1.18	1.32	1.45	1.70	1.79	2.26	1.2
Average rate payments as percentage of average GHI in each range:													
3 Gross rates, per cent of GHI	7.4	6.0	5.8	4.6	3.9	3.5	3.3	2.7	2.4	2.4	2.1	1.7	2.5
4 Net rates, per cent of GHI	nil	0.6	1.1	1.7	2.5	2.4	2.5	2.4	2.2	2.3	2.0	1.7	1.9
Average rate payments as percentage of average disposable income (DI) of households in each range of GHI:													
5 Gross rates, per cent of DI	7.5	6.2	6.0	4.9	4.4	4.1	3.9	3.3	2.9	2.9	2.6	2.2	3.1
6 Net rates, per cent of DI	nil	0.6	1.1	1.9	2.8	2.7	2.9	2.9	2.7	2.8	2.5	2.2	2.3
7 Percentage of all households in each income range	12.2	5.8	4.5	4.6	3.9	3.9	4.1	8.9	8.9	9.3	14.5	19.5	100

Source: De interview Survey, April-May 1975. Reproduced from Layfield (1976). Table 36.

TABLE 6.3 *Average payments of rates and national taxation by range of Gross Household Income (Great Britain April-May 1975)*

				Range of Gross Household Income (GHI) per week						
		to £20	to £30	to £40	to £50	to £60	to £70	to £80	to £100	over £100	All households
1	Mean GHI £ per week	15.6	24.7	34.9	45.0	55.0	65.0	75.0	89.3	136.2	68.1
2	Percentage of all households in each income range	12.2	10.3	8.5	8.0	8.9	8.9	9.3	14.5	19.5	100
3	Income tax £ per week	0.2	0.5	2.4	4.5	7.3	9.0	11.6	14.1	28.7	10.8
3a	per cent of GHI	1.4	2.1	6.9	10.0	13.2	13.9	15.5	15.8	21.0	15.9
4	National indirect taxes £ per week	2.3	4.1	5.8	7.1	8.4	9.3	10.5	12.2	18.4	9.9
4a	per cent of GHI	14.5	16.4	16.8	15.8	15.2	14.3	14.0	13.7	13.5	14.5
5	Total national taxes £ per week (lines 3 and 4)	2.5	4.6	8.2	11.6	15.6	18.3	22.1	26.4	47.0	20.7
5a	per cent of GHI	15.8	18.5	23.7	25.8	28.4	28.2	29.5	29.5	34.5	30.4
6	Net rates £ per week	nil	0.2	0.7	1.1	1.3	1.5	1.7	1.8	2.3	1.3
6a	per cent of GHI	nil	0.8	2.1	2.5	2.4	2.2	2.3	2.0	1.7	1.9
7	National taxes plus net rates £ per week	2.5	4.8	9.0	12.7	17.0	19.8	23.8	28.1	49.3	22.0
7a	per cent of GHI	15.8	19.3	25.8	28.3	30.8	30.4	31.8	31.5	36.2	32.2

Source: Re-interview Survey, 1975, and, for estimates of indirect taxes, 'Economic Trends', December 1974, 'Financial Statement and Budget Report', 1974-5 and 1975-6. Reproduced from Layfield (1976), Table 38.

provides for the hardship which might otherwise be imposed
on the poorest. Finally, although rates bear no relation to
the services enjoyed by the ratepayer, it is a characteristic
of a tax (as opposed to a fee or a charge) that it is not a
payment related to services provided.

OTHER OBJECTIONS

The objections set out at 1, 3, 4 and 8 above have largely been
answered in the preceding paragraphs when the total tax bill
of the occupiers is considered as a whole. Numbers 2, 9 and
10 could be remedied by valuing dwellings to capital values
where there is adequate evidence, although similar dwellings
would still have different values because that would be the
market evidence. If it is desired that the same type of dwelling
has the same assessment irrespective of its location, one must
depart from valuation and go to some formula, based on area
and other factors, which perforce will be arbitrary. The infre-
quency of valuations could be remedied if government allowed
revaluations to take place at set intervals and technical problems could be solved by the introduction of computers into the
Valuation Office. (The present position is the antithesis of the
last in that the Local Government Planning and Land Act 1980
has abolished the requirement to have revaluations quinquen-
nially; and the Inland Revenue Valuation Office computer project
was closed down half-way through its implementation stage in
June 1979 on the cancellation of the 1982 revaluation.) Objections 5 and 6 are philosophical and the same objections can be
levied against many other taxes. Indeed, to be acceptable a tax
does not have to fit every criterion of perfection - it may have
certain disadvantages and yet be acceptable.

The last two 'charges' (11 and 12) are worthy of further consideration. Buoyancy can be looked at in various ways. Firstly,
a truly buoyant tax is one where revenue grows in line with
Gross Domestic Product like income tax. Secondly, buoyancy
can be considered in terms of Rateable Value (RV) increasing
in line with property values. Thirdly, buoyancy can be measured by the level of the rate in the pound.

Rates do not fit the first aspect of buoyancy. By reason of
(a) infrequent valuations and (b) a basis of valuation, generally
called 'tone', whereby values of new properties in a Valuation
List are inserted at levels of value prevailing when the list
came into force, such buoyancy as is inherently in the system is
artificially restricted. Accordingly, the third aspect is much
to the fore and each year ratepayers see the rate in the pound
increasing.

THE REPRESSED BUOYANCY

The growth in total RV over the past decade has been as follows
(the figures are as at the 1 April of the year just mentioned):

TABLE 6.4 *Rateable values*

Year	Total RV (£m)	% increase over previous year
1970-1	2440.5	–
1971-2	2492.8	2.14
1972-3	2545.9	2.13
1973-4	6583.0	158.57
1974-5	6660.1	1.17
1975-6	6742.2	1.23
1976-7	6809.2	0.99
1977-8	6934.7	1.84
1978-9	7058.0	1.77
1979-80	7181.9	1.75
1980-1	7317.8	1.89
1981-2	7441.2	1.69

Source: Inland Revenue (1980), Table 5.4.

The sharp jump from 1972-3 to 1973-4 was caused by the new
Valuation Lists which came into force on 1 April 1973 on levels
current at that time, whereas the 1972-3 list was still reflecting
1963 values. The rate of increase in RV is only about 2 per cent
per annum and is caused by new building and improvements to
the existing stock whereas Layfield observed (1976, 14.14)
'in reality property values also increase with inflation – over the
past 10 years at a rate of 10% a year'. Thus the policy of 'tone
valuations' has restricted the increase in rateable values
between April 1973 and April 1980 to some £730 million whereas
the true increase in value is probably 10 times that amount.
Whereas 'tone' is an excellent idea when revaluations take place
at short intervals, it has a dampening effect when valuation
lists have to last for twice as long as the period for which they
were designed or even longer.

CHANGES IN THE PROPORTIONS OF TOTAL RV BETWEEN DOMESTIC AND OTHER SECTORS

As at 1 April 1973 of £6,583 million RV, domestic property
accounted for £3,234 million (49.12 per cent of the total), commercial property for £1,692.5 million (25.7 per cent) and industrial £817.8 million (12.42 per cent). (Public utilities, educational,

entertainment, Crown and miscellaneous property has been
excluded.)

As at 1 April 1981 of £7,441.2 million RV, domestic property
accounted for £3,630.5 million (48.78 per cent), commercial
property for £1,857.8 million (24.96 per cent) and industrial
for £787.2 million (10.57 per cent).

The average RV of a domestic, a commercial and an industrial
property at the earlier date was £190.9, £573.8 and £7,811
respectively; whereas at the latter date they were £194.4,
£590.3 and £7,366.5. It will thus be seen that whereas the
domestic and commercial sector averages have shown marginal
increases, the industrial sector average has fallen some 5.7 per
cent.

When it comes to payment of rate bills, it must be realised that
domestic ratepayers have been cushioned by domestic rate relief
which amounts generally to 18.5 pence in the pound. Thus if a
householder is paying rates of virtually one pound per pound
of RV, the shopkeeper or industrialist in that area is paying
£1.18½ per pound of RV.

TABLE 6.5 *Make-up of total rate income 1960-1 — 1980-1*
(England and Wales)

	Total rate income £ million	Amount contributed by industry and commerce £ million	Proportion of total rate income contributed by industry and commerce %
1960-61	694.1	234.3	33.76
1961-62	744.6	253.4	34.03
1962-63	828.4	283.3	34.20
1963-64	920.1	355.5	38.64
1964-65	988.1	370.3	37.48
1965-66	1,128.4	417.1	36.96
1966-67	1,262.9	463.9	36.73
1967-68	1,352.2	494.4	36.56
1968-69	1,450.8	528.2	36.41
1969-70	1,594.8	578.6	36.28
1970-71	1,747.2	632.3	36.19
1971-72	2,036.8	735.1	36.09
1972-73	2,323.9	837.8	36.05
1973-74	2,632.0	948.0	36.02
1974-75	3,424.0	1,272.7	37.17
1975-76	4,478.0	1,645.7	36.75
1976-77	4,904.0	1,773.3	36.16
1977-78	5,431.0	1,927.5	35.49
1978-79	5,893.0	2,073.2	35.18
1979-80	6,848.0	2,409.1	35.18
1980-81	8,512.0	2,994.5	35.18

Source: 'Hansard' (1980, 24 July, cols 377-8).

Surprisingly, in view of the above, the proportion of total rate income contributed by commerce and industry has a fairly close correlation with the proportion of total RV attributable to commerce and industry as Table 6.5 shows.

THE ROLE OF THE COMMERCIAL INDUSTRIAL SECTOR

This sector has no vote in local affairs and the only way it can show its displeasure with a local authority (apart from the understandably noisy political lobbying of recent times) is to close down and move elsewhere. Even then, if its premises remain empty, liability for rates may continue. In any event the remedy may be too drastic – a cutting off of the nose to spite the face. On the other hand, the domestic sector is vociferous and can express its views through the ballot box. Thus until recently most of the study into the impact of rates has concentrated on householders. The bulk of the evidence presented to the Layfield Committee concerned domestic rates. With the recession of the 1980s interest is now beginning to be concentrated on the non-domestic sector as industrialists become more cost conscious and realise that they may be being penalised, because disenfranchised.

In the domestic sector the person who pays the rate bill has to find the money from his own pocket. In the non-domestic sector it may be possible to shift the burden onwards; for instance, rates on a shop may be passed on to the customer in higher prices at the counter. The prevailing incidence of non-domestic rates may well be very uncertain.

At a seminar set up by the Centre for Environmental Studies on the subject of 'The Impact of Rates on Industry and Commerce' Douglas Mair pointed out

that low income households are tending to consume relatively high proportions of goods and services on which non-domestic rates (NDR) tax rates are relatively high, e.g. fuel, light and power, food and services and relatively small proportion of goods and services on which NDR rates are relatively low, e.g. tobacco, durable household goods and other goods. Similarly high income households are tending to consume relatively high proportions of goods and services on which NDR rates are relatively low and relatively low proportions of goods and services on which NDR tax rates are relatively high.

The same point is made by C.D. Foster:

Rates on non-domestic ratepayers will in the long run be passed on in higher prices, and will become another form of indirect taxation. Indirect taxation is regressive. Thus the net distributional impact of non-domestic rates will be regressive, the more so the more the super-rating. In the long run this could offset the effects of rate rebates. (Foster et al., 1980, p. 418)

PLANT-INTENSIVE PROPERTIES

The rate bill on an industrial property is calculated by multiplying the rate in the pound by the net annual value. This is defined in the General Rate Act 1967 Section 19(3) as

> an amount equal to the rent at which it is estimated the hereditament might reasonably be expected to let from year to year if the tenant undertook to pay all usual tenants rates and taxes and to bear the cost of the repairs and insurance and the other expenses, if any, necessary to maintain the hereditament in a state to command that rent.

Besides the 'property' itself, Section 21 of the same Act provides:

> (a) subject to any order under sub-section (5) of this section, all such plant or machinery in or on the hereditament as belongs to any of the classes set out in the statement for the time being having effect under sub-section (4) of this Section shall be deemed to be part of the hereditament.

Schedule 3 of the same Act lists the 5 classes of plant deemed to be part of the hereditament, e.g. machinery and plant used mainly or exclusively for the generation, storage, primary transformation or main transmission of power; heating and cooling plant; lifts used for passengers; such part of plant and machinery including gasholders, blast furnaces, coke ovens, water towers with tanks as is in the nature of a building or structure. Furthermore, a statement has been issued setting out the types of machinery and plant falling within the 5 classes specified in Schedule 3 - The Plant and Machinery (Rating) Order 1960 (SI 1960 No. 122) as amended.
It will be apparent that there is not usually market evidence as to the rent at which a property containing such plant and machinery would let from year to year and over the years a method of valuation has grown up whereby interest on capital value can be looked at as prima facie evidence to indicate the rent a tenant would pay.
The valuation method has been described as having five stages:
1 estimate the cost of construction;
2 deduct to allow for age obsolescence and any other factors to arrive at 'effective capital value' (ECV);
3 estimate the cost of the site;

4 apply the appropriate rate of interest;
5 consider whether the calculation does really represent the
rent the tenant would pay and adjust further as necessary.
The matter of valuation by 'tone' has been mentioned earlier. If
a ratepayer 'objects' to his current rating assessment he will
make a 'proposal' to reduce it. Two valuations require to be
made:
1 as the 'tone' valuation;
2 as the valuation at levels prevailing at the date of the ratepayers proposal.
If a complex industrial hereditament is now considered where
part is functioning normally but other parts are working at very
low capacity due to trade recession, which has grown up since
the Valuation List was published (and is thus not a factor
allowed to be reflected in the 'tone' valuation) it will be seen
that:
(a) the tone valuation is probably the existing one which the
ratepayer considers too high;
(b) the current cost of the plant will be vastly increased compared with costs when the 1973 valuation list was being prepared. Interest rates are also vastly higher.
Thus if a substantial part of a factory is beneficially occupied,
the increased value of that part valued under (b) above will
outweigh any adjusting factor allowed under (5) above on the
remainder, so that although as a whole the value of the works
has declined, it is not possible to secure any rating reduction.
   On the other hand, where there is possibly only one process
carried on and it has declined, it will be possible to prove that
valuation (b) is less than (a). Accordingly, there are cases
where the existing system penalises certain industrial properties
which have a diversity of uses.

REPORT ON NON-DOMESTIC RATES

Shell UK Ltd (Small Business Unit) commissioned Coopers &
Lybrand Associates Ltd, Management and Economic Consultants,
to produce a report on Non-Domestic Rates with particular
reference to small firms. The forty-page study plus Appendices
cannot be summed up with justice in a few words, but some of
the points made are referred to below. (A word of caution is
required. Professor C.D. Foster, whose book is mentioned
above, was also concerned with the Centre for Environmental
Studies seminar already mentioned and he led the Coopers &
Lybrand's research team. Thus, to some degree, one may be
getting only one view presented from three different sources.)
   The report points out that published statistics do not directly
identify small businesses, but they estimate the number of
these as being in the region of 750,000. The authors believe
that small firms in service industries are particularly affected
by high rates due possibly to the fact that they use a lot of

accommodation pro rata to their output.

   Dealing with the future of rates, the report did not detect
any strong pressure to see non-domestic rates abolished, unless
domestic rates were abolished. It strongly criticises the postponement of the 1982 revaluation and the section in the Local
Government Planning and Land Act 1980 which removes the
necessity for quinquennial evaluations.

   It notes the anomalies that may now exist which are due to
the different rates of increase of various commercial classes
(e.g. shops, offices and industrial property) in money rent
terms, and when rents are adjusted for inflation as evidenced
by the 'Investors Chronicle' Hillier Parker Rent Index. This
is illustrated by Table 6 from the report, reproduced here as
Table 6.6.

TABLE 6.6 *Commercial and industrial rents: Great Britain*

(a) Indices of money rents

Index	1973	1974	1975	1976	1977 May	Nov.	1978 May	Nov.	1979 May
'Investors Chronicle' Hillier Parker Rent Index (all commercial property)	100	117	121	124	131	137	147	158	175
Shops	100	117	124	133	144	154	171	191	216
Offices	100	112	111	107	109	112	119	125	136
Industrial	100	130	149	162	178	186	192	204	228

(b) Indices of rents adjusted for inflation

Index	1973	1974	1975	1976	1977 May	Nov.	1978 May	Nov.	1979 May
All commercial property	100	101	84	74	67	68	70	72	75
Shops	100	101	85	80	74	76	81	88	92
Offices	100	97	77	64	56	55	57	57	58
Industrial	100	113	102	97	91	92	91	93	98

Note: The 'Investors Chronicle' Hillier Parker Rent Indices are based on data on market
rental levels, measured for different types of commercial property at 189 locations through
Great Britain.
Source: Table 7, 'Investors Chronicle' Hillier Parker Rent Index. (See Table 8 Shell UK Ltd.
(Small Business Unit) Report on Non-Domestic Rates, February 1980).

The report also draws attention to regional variations for shops,
offices and industry in four regions, again using the same
indices.

TABLE 6.7 *Regional variations in commercial and industrial rents*
(a) Shops Index (1973 = 100)

Region	1973	1976	1979 (May)
London	100	127	228
South-East	100	145	218
Midlands	1100	123	100
North	100	135	232

(b) Office Index (1973 = 100)

Region	1973	1976	1979 (May)
London	100	76	104
South-East	100	142	163
Midlands	100	130	157
North	100	155	206

(c) Industrial Index (1973 = 100)

Region	1973	1976	1979 (May)
London	100	154	230
South-East	100	154	213
Midlands	100	155	230
North	100	155	226

Source: Table 8, 'Investors Chronicle', Hillier Parker Rent Index.

The report comments:

In the case of *shops*, those in prime locations have performed something like twice as well as those in other locations. Thus lack of revaluation is operating to the dis-
advantage of those occupying smaller shop premises in
secondary locations. To the extent that the final incidence
of rates is on the landlord this acts as a hidden subsidy to
landlords of favoured sites.

In the case of *offices*, rent movements have been more
uniform but even so significant divergencies can be dis-
cerned. For example, rent levels in the City of London are
comparable with those prevailing in 1973 although in the
West End office rents have approximately doubled in the
same period. Whereas in Birmingham office rents have more
than doubled, in Bristol the increase has only been about
50%. The longer such divergent trends continue without
being reflected in rateable values the greater the inequity

in the distribution of the rate burden.

In the industrial property market again there are diver-
gences. Whereas modern and well placed factories and ware-
houses have shown good rental growth, older and less well
placed properties have shown little or no growth. In the
latter category are industrial properties in declining inner
city areas and in areas affected by industrial contraction
(e.g. steel and shipbuilding areas).

THE LOCAL GOVERNMENT PLANNING AND LAND ACT 1980

With the current interest in the plight of small businesses a few
measures have been introduced to alleviate the burden on such
occupations. Thus whereas domestic rate relief is at present
received by domestic occupiers and some relief given to those
in mixed user properties where the domestic value is more than
a half of the total; relief in future will be given in varying
degrees where the domestic value falls between one eighth and
the former 50 per cent limit (Sect. 33).

Again, whereas at present domestic occupiers can pay rates
by instalments but not commercial ratepayers; the latter will
in future have this right within certain rateable value limits
(Sect. 34). Furthermore, if there is a revaluation which increases
the burden on an occupier and he appeals against his assessment the Secretary of State may make an order allowing part of
the increase to remain unpaid until the appeal is settled.

The much publicised 'Enterprise Zones' have been designated
and within these there will be no liability to pay rates except
for domestic properties and public utility undertakings. It will
be of interest to see whether any real benefit will accrue to
occupiers or whether rents within the zones will rise to the
levels of rents plus rates outside the zones, thus putting the
benefit into the pocket of the landlord. Assessments for these
properties will appear in Valuation Lists and the Secretary of
State will give grants to compensate for the rates lost. This
money coming from the taxpayers at large is a further example
of giving piecemeal relief, i.e. that one ratepayer's gain has to
be paid for by those not relieved. Historically, this tinkering
with the system normally leads in time to a revolt by the mass
of the ratepayers and a clean sweep revaluation when all reliefs
of this nature are withdrawn and values put back to market
levels.

Two small improvements have been made to the valuation process (if a revaluation is ordered). Firstly, the Secretary of
State may order that valuations be made as at an antecedent
date. This will ensure that all 'Valuation Lists' are at the same
levels of values. Hitherto Valuation Officers have endeavoured
to project valuations forward to the date of the coming into
force of the Valuation List, but in times of soaring inflation
have succeeded in varying degrees. Regrettably, however, the

abovementioned 'Valuation Lists' may be lists of specific types of properties only and different dates could be specified for different types.

Secondly, whereas now, a number of commercial classes such as shops, offices, hotels, cinemas and pubs are valued to gross value (i.e. assuming the tenant pays rates but the landlord pays for repairs), in any future revaluation these will be valued to net annual value (i.e. assuming the tenant both pays the rates and the cost of repairs). This basis is closer to that on which much commercial property is let and will thus make the assessments more realistic to the layman. It will cut out a stage in the revaluation process whereby scale deductions were made (for the Inland Revenue these have minor manpower saving implications!). On the other hand, it may give rise to litigation on the method of application of the new basis.

It is Sect. 28 of the Act that makes the most fundamental change in the practice of rating. Hitherto the requirement has been that revaluations should take place every five years (General Rate Act 1967 Sect. 68). Although this objective has not been achieved, the postponements each required the sanction of parliament. The situation has now been completely reversed so that new valuation lists are only to come into force as and when the Secretary of State may specify.

Whereas previously all property was valued at the time of a revaluation, Sect. 30 enabled the Secretary of State to order a revaluation of specific classes of hereditaments and to order non-valued classes to be adjusted by factors or divisors.

The basis is thus capable of much manipulation instead of being an independent reflection of open market rental values. The capability of putting off revaluations, perpetuates anomalies caused by shifting patterns of value, former errors and the effects of Sect. 21 of the Local Government Act 1974 referred to later.

THE NEED FOR A REVALUATION

Although the government are desirous of abolishing rates, no alternative source of finance has been discovered by them which would be compatible with a local democracy. As Brian Hill pointed out: 'This search for an alternative has proved illusory to date and is likely to remain so for a number of years especially when it is borne in mind that the cost would be equivalent to a rise in income tax by $5\frac{1}{2}$p in the £ or a rise in VAT of some 5%' (Hill, 1980).

If one assumes that the 1973 Valuation List showed the correct relativities between classes of properties, between individual properties in a region and between similar properties in different regions, it is obvious that by now there is a serious imbalance. Examples of this have been given above and are further illustrated when one looks at the Hillier Parker Index for (say) shops and offices.

TABLE 6.8 *Hillier Parker Index converted to base 100 at 1973*

Shops	May 1980	May 1981
All shops	246.6	256.5
Central London	323.2	275.5
Inner Suburbs London	164.5	168.2
Outer Suburbs London	179.7	196.2
Suburban London	174.8	187.4
London	242.8	227.6

Offices	May 1980	May 1981
All offices	156.6	176.1
Central City	86.8	95.2
Fringe City	94.9	105.4
West End	156.6	160.0
Holborn/Marylebone	150.8	155.3
Central London	112.2	119.3
Suburban London	169.7	209.1
London	123.5	136.7

The many changes in relativities point to the need for a revaluation. Consider the outcry that would arise if rates of income tax had risen because the figures on which people were required to pay in 1980 and beyond were their income in 1973!

The imbalance is compounded in the case of dwellings where minor improvements have taken place since 1 April 1974 which would add £30 or less gross value to the assessment. Such improvements have escaped rate liability due to the provisions of Section 21 of the Local Government Act 1974 so that identical dwellings next door to each other can have quite different rating assessments purely by the chance that one carried out its improvement after 1 April 1974 and the other prior thereto. The loss to rating authorities by reason of this provision is estimated to be some £25 million of domestic rateable value and is rising continuously. A further anomaly has been detected between the assessments of houses and flats. Rental evidence for the former was scarce and valuers tended to under-assess whereas rental evidence for flats being more plentiful, their assessments tend to be at full 1972-3 levels.

Yet another anomaly, arising for the same reason - lack of evidence - is the apparent tendency for more valuable dwellings to be rated pro rata lower than less valuable ones. Again, there was limited evidence at the lower end of the scale but virtually none at the top end.

In the industrial field the difficulty of correcting the valuations of composite plants has already been pointed out. In a revaluation the correct relativities can be established between the sluggish sections of the economy, e.g. steel, and the more prosperous ones, e.g. drugs.

In the commercial sector, introduction of new technology has caused changes in work patterns. Microfilming and computers cause contraction of filing rooms and storage space. Improved communications have led firms to have smaller central offices with sub-offices dispersed to areas where rents are lower. This in turn has led to higher rents out of London, but this matter cannot be reflected in valuations due to the 'tone' provisions. On a revaluation the whole can be put right.

Since the last Valuation List shopping patterns have changed. Many shopping precincts have been created, drawing trade from one area of a city to another. The falls in value have often been reflected in reduced assessments but not always the increases in other areas. Without a general revaluation it is difficult to correct for these changes and in particular to limit the revisions to practical proportions. Additionally, out of town superstores and hypermarkets have pulled trade in some areas right outside the town to the former 'green fields' site.

These types of changes can be reflected (by virtue of Section 20 General Rate Act 1967) in the assessment of public houses, but not, for instance, in the case of petrol filling stations which are valued on a somewhat similar basis. As opposed to the situation in England and Wales, Scotland has virtually had quinquennial valuations. There are, therefore, anomalies between the two sides of the border.

The bulk of the appeals following a revaluation arise from changes in relativities. If these changes were constantly being reflected, there would be public acceptances of them. It is when there is a long delay between revaluations that the changes are most marked. This leads to a large number of appeals, the cost of which falls on taxpayers as a whole. As a practical matter, the more the uncertainty about rates, the more the staff capable of doing a revaluation leave government service for other fields or retire and are not replaced. The time will not be far distant when there will not be a trained workforce capable of doing a revaluation if the government orders one. For all of the above reasons, a new revaluation is long overdue and should be put in hand without delay.

POSTSCRIPT

In December 1981 the government published a Green Paper entitled 'Alternatives to Domestic Rates' (1981). In fact the title is scarcely suitable, for the paper sets out an extremely good case for keeping domestic rates. As many earlier reports have indicated, other local taxes have marked weaknesses and, in fact, like the Layfield Report before it, the Green Paper inclines to the view that the only conceivable alternative would be a local income tax. Layfield, indeed, saw LIT as a supplement to rates.

The thought of more than one local tax is examined by the government, though, as it is pointed out, the number of permutations is very large and it would not be practical to identify and examine them all. Nevertheless, the Green Paper states (para. 12.2) that 'such permutations would be expensive to run because more than one set of administration and compliance costs would be involved'.

A very real problem for central government in combinations of local taxes would be the difficulties in the way of financial control and there would also be a considerable problem in administering the grant system.

In January 1982 Mr Tom King, the responsible Minister in the Department of the Environment, made a number of statements which were of considerable importance. He said:

(a) that the Green Paper was backed up by a clear commitment by the government to reform;
(b) that the government has no intention of altering the balance between domestic and non-domestic rates;
(c) that the government would measure any alternatives to the rating system against an improved rating system;
(d) that legislation would be forthcoming before the end of this parliament.

In February 1982 the Environment Committee of the House of Commons embarked upon an 'Enquiry into Methods of Financing Local Government in the Context of the Government's Green Paper (Cmnd 8449)' and a report was published in July 1982 and concluded:

(i) The abolition of the domestic rating system would not command widespread support and would not be justified
(ii) The continuing decline in the size of the private rented sector precluded any increase in evidence to support a valuation on a rental basis and a revaluation based on current rental basis was no longer feasible
(iii) The Government should take an early decision that the next revaluation should be carried out in the basis of capital values
(iv) Capital valuations to be assessed by the District Valuer, with banding to ensure that market values are taken into consideration and introduced as soon as it is practical to do so
(v) A regular statutory revaluation of property is necessary and it should be at three yearly intervals
(vi) The Government's view that a range of local taxes (duties on petrol, alcohol or tobacco, vehicle excise duty, licences for the sale of alcohol, or petrol and a local payroll tax) have no place in financing local authority expenditure is accepted
(vii) No support for a local sales tax, which should not be pursued

(viii) A Poll Tax, even at a low level, should not be introduced

(ix) A LIT would ensure local accountability and a substantial yield: a LIT should be examined in depth by government. A wide measure of political support would be necessary for its introduction. Little evidence was received that this support would be forthcoming

(x) Government should give early consideration to LIT and begin a detailed examination of methods of implementation and administration

(xi) LIT fully integrated with the national income tax system or LIT assessment and collection by local authorities based on information about incomes provided by the Inland Revenue are the most likely systems to be found suitable

(xii) Assigned revenues should not be adopted as an alternative to domestic rates

(xiii) In the absence of documented evidence from the Department, the Committee is persuaded by the overwhelming evidence that the costs of education should not be transferred to central government

(xiv) The introduction of an education block grant is as unacceptable as the transfer of the costs of education to central government and would require full and prior public debate

(xv) Yield from a new local tax (LIT) should be used to reduce central government grant, thus encouraging local government accountability and autonomy

(xvi) Government should reconsider the nature and extent of its financial controls over local authorities

(xvii) Government should undertake detailed investigation of the case for abolishing de-rating of agricultural and other buildings

(xviii) If non-domestic rates are retained, a revaluation should take place soon

(xix) Any reform of the domestic rating system will increase the demand for changes in the non-domestic rating system.

We are still waiting for the Government's decisions. Indeed on 17 January 1983 Mr Giles Shaw MP, Parliamentary Under Secretary, replying to a question from Mr Ken Woolmer MP for Batley and Morley about plans for commerical revaluation, said no more than 'we shall announce our decision as soon as possible.'

So after all the promises about reform we have another government paper proving beyond any real doubt that there is no alternative to the rating system. Reform there should certainly be, by way of a move towards a system based upon capital values as the Layfield Committee recommended. There should be as well a revaluation of non-domestic property. Unless urgent decisions are taken on these matters there is the risk of the rating system withering away to the very considerable detriment of both democratic local government and the services which it provides.

Pensions, wealth and the extension of inequality

Mike Reddin

In contemporary Britain there are a variety of forces (none of them mystical - although most of them uncontrolled or unintended) which are widening the existing disparities of income and wealth. They are sometimes conspicuous, but often function invisibly; with or without evident motive they result in an increasing polarisation of resources: they are never inevitable but result from the interaction of particular policies with particular settings. These interactions and their consequences for pensions form the subject of this chapter.

Most dramatic shifts in the pension world stem from policy rather than social or demographic changes. But, whilst the 'natural' changes are slow, and we notice them less, they may be none the less significant: if the distance between cause and effect is great we may simply have to look harder for the connections. In what follows I try to identify some of these linkages. I begin by exploring the links between pensions and earnings, the consequences of earnings-related contributions and benefits, before going on to identify the many non-income factors which influence the redistributive effects of pension schemes. I conclude with a brief addendum on the peculiar significance of wealth for the elderly.

PENSIONS AND WAGES: SOME CONSEQUENCES OF EARNINGS-RELATED BENEFITS

At this stage I want to draw attention to some of the links between the value of pensions and wage differences.

This year in Britain more money will be paid out to retired pensioners than ever before. There are more pensioners and the amount of state, occupational and 'private' individual pensions will be absolutely and proportionately greater than ever.

At the same time, their opposite numbers – the 'active workforce' – are in decline and are insecure. Many have recently
joined the ranks of the unemployed, the 'displaced persons' of
peace: more may follow. Few people today will talk with certainty
of their job or career future. In contrast, the income position
of the pensioner seems to have become more secure. Over the
past twenty years governments have committed themselves
increasingly, first by word and then by legislation, to formally
securing the pensioners' relative income standing. Where the
wage earners have still been required to make their way unsup-
ported by government guarantees – indeed where wage earners
have rejected any socialisation of wages and clung to the wage
market – this relative shift in security has gained in importance.
There was a time when the thriving dynamics of wages were
contrasted with the declining fixed income of the pensioner:
today, we are as likely to find enmity towards the dynamisation
of the latter when contrasted with the comparative decline and
insecurity of the former.

Many nations conduct wage and pension bargaining in the
same breath. In formal national negotiations the employer and
employee share out some part of the national wealth which
should go to each and the relative share of pensioner and worker
arise as the result of more or less conscious choice. Britain,
retaining its love of a fight, continues with disconnected punch-
ups in the labour market: one employer confronts his or her
workforce on irregular occasions; sometimes federations of
employers face associated groups of employees. The virility of
each party is proved by their willingness to call the other's
bluff. Government reinforces these macho tactics with its own
employees – whether consultant surgeons or manual labourers.

The net result is an enormous range of original wage incomes
but, most important, a range that has survived more or less
unchanged for a century at least (Piachaud, 1978). It is to these
disparities that we have increasingly linked the contribution
and benefit formulae of both state and occupational pensions.

EARNINGS-RELATED CONSEQUENCES

In recent years both state and occupational pension systems
have moved towards earnings-related benefits. State pensions
have moved from flat-rate contributions and flat-rate benefits
via the 'minimalist' earnings-relation of contributions and benefits in the graduated pension scheme from 1961 to 1975. That
particular piece of earnings-relation was built on top of the flat
rate system. We also saw the gradual extension of earnings-
related contributions (contracted out or not) during this period,
but the retention of fundamentally flat-rate benefits. Not until
1975 do earnings-related contributions become the norm (at
least for the employed) and then it is not until 1978 that such
contributions are reflected in earnings-related additions to

future pensions. From the vantage point of the early 1980s it
will be many years before even the highest paid have earnings-
related ('additional components') as great as their flat-rate
'basic amounts'.

In the world of occupational pensions there have been similar
earnings-related trends. Whilst many had enjoyed some earnings-
relation from the start (such as those within the Civil Service
scheme), others had been less generously treated. Whilst
contributions were usually proportional to wages or wage bands
(and always with the emphasis on the employer's role as contributor), benefits were less predictable - if not discretionary.
Some schemes offered so many pounds of benefit per year of
service: most had offered money purchase arrangements, with
'contribution-determined' pensions reflecting the amount paid in
(by employees and/or their employers) and any investment
earnings which such savings generated. Only recently has it
become the norm to have final salary earnings-related schemes,
usually jointly financed by employee and employer contributions,
typically in the ratio of one to two. In short, at state and company level the move has been to make both contributions and
benefits increasingly related to the individual's former earnings.

In turn, the earnings-base to which benefits are related has
also shifted. It has done so indirectly in the occupational
schemes as they moved from money purchase, 'year-by-year'
arrangements, to the 'final salary' model. In contrast, the
state scheme has shifted by way of 'graduated' money purchase
to an earnings base of the average of the 'best twenty years'
moderated by reference to changes in national average earnings. The potential redistributive effects of these various
formulae is very important. However, I want now to explore the
extent to which it is the earnings-related base, or *other* variables, which account primarily for the redistributive effects of
pension schemes.

PENSIONS AND REDISTRIBUTION

A redistributive study must pose three pairs of inter-related
questions. From whom and to whom do resources move? How
much is moved from whom and to whom? And, for how long does
such to-ing and fro-ing occur? The momentary distribution of
wealth may be of little significance: we will want to identify
from where it comes and to whom it moves and what its movement means. Some of the movements are abrupt whilst others
are drawn out over long periods.

Few redistributions are 'balanced' in terms of time: there is
usually a different time scale on the input and the output side
of the equation. A large win on the premium bonds may come
after many years of monthly investments or could arise after
the first purchase. The sudden prize will 'come from' a large
number of bond purchasers who have invested varied amounts

over varying numbers of years. Similarly, a lifetime of monthly
savings can be instantly lost - terminated by death before
retirement. In a pooled insurance scheme such savings will go
to others who survive, over many years. Many years of tax-
paying may be 'balanced' by one brief episode of intensive
hospital care. In contrast, the first week's work can culminate
in an industrial accident leaving someone dependent on social
benefits for the rest of their days. So, the time scales over
which redistributions occur have two potentially distinct dimensions: the duration of the inputs and the duration of the outputs may not be the same; they may or may not be simultaneous.
   The point of these particular ruminations is that pensions
offer more than the usual potential for disparities between
inputs and outputs. For instance, many of the men who retire
this year will have been in the wage market (as earners, taxpayers and contributors) for fifty years: on average they will
be pensioners for twelve years. Many other men will retire
this year who will only have been in the wage market (taxpayers, etc.) for some forty years: on average their life
expectancy will see them as pensioners for something more than
twelve years. Some will die just before age 65: others will live
for twenty years or more. Their respective 'rates of return'
will vary accordingly.
   Having posed the six-dimension formula, I want now to
attempt to describe in more detail the entries that should be
made in each dimension. For those who like solutions to quizzes,
I should point out that I reach no definitive resolution of the
equation. However, I do try to spell out the elements from which
an answer could be constructed. Since any answer will necessarily depend on many assumptions I try to make them clear,
or suggest their boundaries, at each stage.

THE INPUTS: WHO PAYS?

The first step is to identify the dramatis personae: they
include, conspicuously, employees and employers who make
payments called national insurance contributions. Whilst not all
of this money is devoted to retirement pensions, our concern
here is with the origin of these resources. Some of the actors
in this drama are no more than the bearers of messages. The
employer's contribution, discussed at some length later in this
chapter, is effectively a 'detached' part of an individual's wage:
we could thus express it as an employee's contribution made by
way of an intermediary (the employer). But, however ascribed
initially, both the employee and employer contributions can be
traced through to the point where wages and all labour costs
are derived from company sales. It is the sale of the tin of
beans, the can of paint, the Ford Cortina, or the services of
hairdresser, solicitor or surgeon which are resolved by way of
a consumer's purchases. In the final analysis only individuals

pay taxes: all roads lead to the consumer of products or of
services.

The consumer/taxpayer may be an individual buying a car
or a private company buying one for a sales representative
(a cost moved on to their product purchasers). The car may be
bought by a public agency: here the incidence of such costs
will be determined by the source of the revenues which finance
that agency. If the National Health Service meets its bills with
the private builder or with the private pharmaceutical company
from taxes, then the transfer effect depends on the incidence
of those taxes. If costs are met from 'user charges', then
(assuming these are not moved on) they fall directly on consumers. If met from public borrowing, then they are met via
'the source' of the loan repayments - which might be further
taxes or further borrowing. (We return later to this discussion
of incidence when we focus attention on the inputs to occupational pension schemes.)

HOW MUCH IS PAID IN?

There are several problems in any attempt to quantify inputs
to pensions - problematic in the sense that it is sometimes hard
to set off Mr A's personal contributions over the years with his
personal pension benefits at the end. The inputs were made
from varying levels of 'current' income over a long period when
money values changed. They were made and earned recognition
under one particular set of rules - which may have a shorter
life than the contributor/beneficiary. The system of pay as you
go (PAYG) deals in hope rather than promises, other than the
promises made by governments. It may be viewed contractually
- I pay now, you pay later - but it is hard to define it as
promisory when those who will pay are quite probably not yet
born. The similarity, perhaps, is that of family and child. There
is no way in which the child can be held liable for the subsequent maintenance of his parents: unless, it is by way of repayment for care and support during youth (and it would be hard
to predict the relative scale of these dependencies: children
might be heavily subsidised whilst the elderly lived lives of
expensive autonomy).

If the scheme is financed by PAYG methods then the transfers
are immediate and, in aggregate, evident. They are current
actions; contributor and beneficiary are contemporaries, visible
to one another. We can measure the quantities which flow across
the space between them. We can note the slow process of infil-
tration - as ageing contributors cross the great divide at pension
age, ceasing to pay in, starting to claim benefit. We can note
each year the new entrants to the contributor population and
the lapsed membership of departing beneficiaries. The formal act
of transfer is ongoing between two (changing) populations, from
current taxpayers (as NI contributors) to current pensioners.

Yet, even within this PAYG process, this is less than the whole story. The largest single component of NI finance comes from employer contributions. These actually 'come from' the consumers, the product purchasers – a group larger than even the current work force (NI contributors): they are indirect taxpayers on a large scale. Further, some 2.5 million pensioners have a combined income from state, occupational and other income sources, which makes them liable for income tax: as such they give to an exchequer which then makes its contribution towards their pensions. It is rare for distributions to be exclusively in one direction.

Where contributions are specifically related to income, we must note that income is not income is not income. Tax and social security systems tend to treat income from different sources in different ways. Income from employment may be treated differently from income from investment. I can be a millionaire but pay no social security contributions if all my income is from investment or many low-paid jobs. The income of married people may be taxable on different terms from the single: the elderly may be taxed differently from the young. It is therefore very likely that the source or form of income receipt will affect its taxability – and thus the extent to which incomes of a particular source or form, actually contribute towards a benefit system. (At the other end of the spectrum, cash benefits may be taxable or non-taxable: as such, their cash value will be modified and their redistributive effects moderated.)

WHO RECEIVES?

Coverage, blanketing-in and transitional effects
There are many variables which can impinge on the redistributive effects of pension schemes, be they public, private or hybrid. The first lies in the choice of the population to be covered. Will it cover all citizens or only working males, or just those in public employment? Will it cover dependants, will it cover any who are currently retired? Will it only affect those who will retire in forty years time or give progressive membership as people accrue benefits year by year? In short, who is to be covered, and at what stage in their lives?

Second, we must distinguish between the redistributive impact of a scheme when it is fully mature and fully operational, and its incremental impact over the years of its implementation. Transitional effects are likely to differ from 'final' effects, not least if the transition involves movement from one established scheme to another. For example, if those already retired are granted some of the new benefit from the outset – a process known as 'blanketing-in' – then there is a major initial redistribution which has substantial short-term implications for the scheme's finances: such benefits will have to be paid for from

current revenue. (This process of 'blanketing-in' is common to
many pension schemes: it may be total with full benefit from the
start or partial, with some fraction of full benefit, perhaps
related to age, or years of membership in some prior scheme.)

Further, the blanketing-in process inevitably brings some
people into full or partial benefit on terms more beneficial than
their successors. That is, people may subsequently be expected
to earn their pension rights (through contributions) over many
years. Blanketing-in has been common in many social security
systems, particularly those stressing the merits of universal
and comprehensive cover. It is also common in occupational
pension schemes either when a new scheme is created for an
existing workforce - with established workers gaining some
credit for service to date - or from the merger of two companies
with different pension schemes: one may be upgraded to the
other. The costs of blanketing may be met in various ways.
They can be met immediately, from taxes in a state scheme or
from an employer's 'lump sum' contribution. Alternatively, in
funded schemes, costs can be spread forward over the future.
Each technique and each source of finance has, as must be
evident, its own distinct redistributive implications.

The extremes of these blanket transfer values can be seen
in a simple example. If a male aged 65 in 1948 had been
blanketed-in to the new state pension scheme, at full benefit,
and was still alive today (aged 99 or over) then he would have
been a pension recipient for some thirty-four years. Compare
that benefit with a worker aged thirty-five in 1948 who contributed for thirty-four years but died on his 65th birthday. On
the one hand we see all benefits at (notionally) no cost and
on the other hand all the contributions with no benefit.

In brief, the coverage of a pension scheme can be varied in
many ways: we may discriminate amongst the members, by sex,
by age, the acknowledgment of dependants, or by the duration
of their membership. As shown here, the decision to admit and
the terms of admission may dramatically differentiate the returns
to particular individuals or to whole age groups admitted 'on
preferential terms'.

So, who receives?
On the face of it this is the simplest question to answer. The
pensioner actually receives the pension and is clearly visible.
However, as with all primary recipients the receipt can be
passed on. If Granny gets the pension - but pays it over to
the daughter with whom she lives, or to the local authority home
in which she is resident, or the private nursing home where
she has settled - then is she appropriately described as the sole
beneficiary? However, having queried the concept of receipt,
I want to proceed on the assumption that pensioners actually
receive pensions and that the pension benefit can be attributed
to them as individuals.

Pension recipients must have several qualities. Of course,

they must be alive, but they must usually meet additional
eligibility conditions. Eligibility may be a function of residence
(in the country which pays the benefit), of contributory
records, of former earnings, or just of membership of the
group - 'people over 65'. The actual level of pension payable
is often a function of all these factors, and many more. The
aggregation of these various conditions at a particular time,
is likely to mean that not all 'of pension age' are eligible for or
in receipt of pensions. Thus, pensioners may be a more or less
select band of the elderly, not always representative of the
age group in question. They may constitute the young old
(because the pension scheme is new) or the old old (because
a scheme which once existed has now been withdrawn). They
will most strongly represent those who have been firmly based
in the labour market - especially as employees: the full-timers
and the males. There are often others who enjoy some benefit
derived from these 'strong men' - dependants of the pensioner
or as widows inheriting a former partner's record (an issue we
explore more fully in a moment).

The UK system also excludes from benefit some people whose
earnings are below a certain level (currently £27 per week).
Whilst there is no obligation to contribute from incomes below
this level, the exclusion can continue with a much higher income.
If the income comes from a series of employments each one of
which pays just short of £27 per week then, for national insurance purposes, these incomes are not aggregated. In theory,
you could have an infinite number of jobs at £26.99 and pay no
contributions - and hence earn no contributory benefits - for
the rest of your working life. (Flat-rate voluntary contributions,
current £3.30 per week could be paid towards flat-rate benefits.)

Thus the pensioners' world comprises the fully 'paid up',
those who have reduced benefits and those who have benefits
largely dependent on others. The extent to which such 'dis-
crepancies' of entitlement are compensated for by supplementary
benefit systems may well shift the final redistributive outcome
of pension schemes. But if we just judge one system, the contributory national insurance pension, it must be apparent that
its beneficiaries do not benefit universally, nor do they enjoy
their benefits for common reasons. And all this, before we
enter the world of earnings-relation.

TRANSFERS BY MARITAL STATUS AND BY SEX

Currently only a minority of people die as 'never married'. Most
men die 'married' most women die as 'widows': increasing numbers die as separated, divorced or as the widow/widower of a
second or subsequent marriage.

Some of these marital status conditions are inter-related with
mortality: the widow lives longer than her single sister, the

divorcee has a shorter life than either. No attempt is made here
to explain these phenomena: it is sufficient to note that the
incidence of such statuses in a society, and within a social
insurance system, may go a long way to determine its redistributive outcomes. Likewise, a change in these status distributions – the numbers who marry, the age at which they do so
(especially age differences between partners), divorce rates
and remarriages, will all modify the redistributive impact of a
particular scheme. Their impact as distributive determinants
will arise either in terms of duration or longevity or because
different rates of benefit are attached to differences in marital
status. (Both single and married pay the same contributions:
they realise very different rates of benefit.) Marriage rates,
the age of the partners within the marriage and the rules concerning the continuation of benefits beyond marriage (through
widowhood, the inheritance of benefits, their division between
several former spouses, etc.) will all moderate distributive
outcomes. I want to explore these outcomes in some detail.

We are starting from the fact that the 'contributory unit' and
the subsequent 'beneficiary unit' are not 'constant bodies'. If
I set aside money for my future, then (allowing for the 'contributions' of interest payers in the interim to my investment
returns) I can trace the flow – over time – made by myself
(now) to myself (then). However, most of us change during
our lives: we alter our marital/dependant/employee/self-
employed statuses throughout our working lives. We may think
up and act out new variations in the future. What effect do such
status changes have on the redistributive outcomes of pension
schemes? I want to attempt an answer by way of some simplified
but reasonable models. I am going to assume a world in which
many other variables remain stable – in which money values, tax
systems, the 'rules of the pension game' do not shift over the
life-span of the pension scheme. (Whilst we are now used to
inflation, we have perhaps concluded that it is the only major
unpredictable in pension provision. However, a change in the
tax treatment or related concessions which protect the pensioner
would dramatically alter the viability of many pension schemes.
It is therefore significant that they are constructed on the
assumption of continuity.)

Let us assume that an employee contribution of 6 per cent
is attributable to the finance of retirement pensions. Imagine
that the worker earns £100 per week. Then £6 per week will be
paid over a working life of, say, forty-five years: 6 x 52 x 45
= £14,040 in total. Now assume that the contributor goes on
to live for twelve years and receives a pension (as a single
person) equal to 30 per cent of previous earnings, i.e. £30 per
week. Thus, total receipts amount to £30 x 52 x 12 = £18,720.
Crudely, on these terms there would be a net gain of £4,680
before death.

In contrast, the same worker but now married, pays in the
same amount but on retirement at 65 would, we assume, receive

a weekly pension for himself and an adult dependant of some
45 per cent of previous gross earnings: i.e. £45 x 52 x 12 =
£28,080 (£9,360 more than his single neighbour and, coincident-
ally, exactly twice the amount contributed). But, beyond the
man's death, after twelve benefit years, we can reasonably
assume another six years survival for his widow which, at the
'single' person's rate means 6 x 52 x £30 = £9,360. Thus their
joint return amounts to a total of £37,440, or, an excess of
benefit over contribution of £23,400. Finally, if instead of
assuming that husband and wife were the same age (and thus
calculating their survival from age 65) we made a more realistic
assumption, that the wife was two years younger than her
husband, then her widow's receipt is extended by another
2 x 52 x £30 = £3,120, a grand total joint benefit of £40,560
and again, an excess of benefit over input of £26,520. The
return would exceed that of the single male pensioner by
£21,840.

These figures are summarised in Table 7.1.

TABLE 7.1 *Pension returns for different types of pensioners*

Contributions £	Benefits £		Excess benefit £
14,040	Single male pensioner (65-77)	18,720	4,680
	Married couple (both 65-77)	28,080	14,040
	Married couple, then widow (77-83)	37,440	23,400
	Married couple, then widow (wife two years younger)	40,560	26,520

Further examples reveal the maximum limits of a scheme based
on these principles. The single male could, having paid his
£14,040 of contributions, drop dead at his 65th birthday party
and enjoy no return at all.

Currently widows' benefits only become payable from age 40
and at full-rate at age 50, so the maximum benefit would in
fact arise where widowhood was at 50 but where 'dependency'
began twelve years earlier; in other words, that she was 38
when he was 65. Then, she would have twelve years as a dependant: £15 x 12 x 52 = £9,360 plus thirty-three years (from 50
to 83) as a widow on the full benefit rate £30 x 33 x 52 =
£51,480, a total of £60,840, which, on top of his twelve-year
pension of £18,720 gives a grand total of £79,560. Suffice it to
say that (without too great a stretch of the imagination) we can
pose extremes in the 'rate of return' for the same contributory

input ranging from nought to some £80,000.

These extremes illustrated arise as a product of marital status and 'dependency' and are independent of the earnings level of the former contributor. If we grafted on the world of earnings-related contributions and benefits we could dramatise the limits yet further. Assume a contributory ceiling roughly comparable to that of today, some seven times the 'basic amount' - the single pension rate: that is in our model, a ceiling of 7 x £30 = £210, for convenience call it £200 per week. Then at a contribution rate of 7.25 per cent the maximum annual contribution would be £754 or, with a full forty-five-year working life, £33,930. Death at age 65 would bring this single male exactly the same return as his non-participating neighbour: nothing.

MALE/FEMALE TRANSFERS

This concept, and its realisation, receives remarkably little attention in popular political discussion of pension systems. Whereas it is widely recognised that women live longer than men within Western European societies - even if this distinction may be changing - the fact has only exceptionally been acknowledged within pension schemes. (This is not to say that 'the fact' should be acknowledged in one particular way.) Women 'on average' live longer than men (about 6.7 years) and within the British pension scheme are allowed to retire and draw benefit (and cease paying contributions) five years earlier than men (at 60 as opposed to 65). This means that there must be a transfer towards women where they have been admitted on much the same terms as men.

Over the years, national insurance schemes have fluctuated in their recognition of this factor. In the state graduated scheme running from 1961-1975 there was a substantial 'compensatory' differential in the contribution rate: women paid £9 per benefit unit in contrast to the £7.50 of men. The differential was officially legitimated solely because women would contribute for a shorter period: the fact that they would receive benefit for longer because of their greater longevity was not (officially) part of the calculation. But, with the demise of the graduated scheme in April 1975, we returned to the more typical model of standard (mainly proportional) contributions coming from single and married, male and female alike. If male and female contributor had similar wage and work histories they enjoyed dissimilar returns: the male could look forward from age 65 to some twelve years of pension receipt, the female could expect from age 60 to receive her pension for more than twenty years.

Conversely, it is also possible to argue that the transfers of many occupational pension schemes have typically moved in the opposite direction - from women to men. If we identify the source of the bulk of contribution income to the pension scheme as deriving from employers' contributions - and if employers

can only practise such generosity when their business is profit-
able, then employees receive their benefits, albeit indirectly
'at the expense' of two discrete sources.

First, since all employees contribute to the company's prosperity but not all are members of the pension scheme there is a
transfer from the 'workforce population' to the 'pension population'. Women are under-represented in the latter, in grades
with no pension cover or excluded as part-time workers: thus,
they contribute but do not benefit. Second, since women
workers have generally higher rates of mobility than men they
lose pension rights (disporportionately) as they change jobs.
When people make such moves and lose or diminish such
accumulated pension rights, they effectively make bequests to
those (predominantly men) who are less mobile. Thus within
the micro-economy of the occupational scheme there are substantial transfers running counter to those which derive from
longevity (Reddin, 1977).

THE OCCUPATIONAL SCHEMES: WHO PAYS?

Up to this point we have considered what can happen within
grand 'universal' schemes - like state retirement pensions;
redistributions governed by the interaction of scheme rules,
their fiscal environment and the social and individual behaviour
(like marriage and longevity) of their members. These factors
it has been argued, rather than the poverty or wealth of
individuals, have done most to account for the redistributions
of British pension schemes. We now turn to look at pensions
with less than universal coverage, the British occupational
schemes.

There are several features which differentiate these occupational pensions from the state retirement pension. First, they
are generally financed by 'advance funding' rather than by
pay as you go. They save the contributions, usually of employer
and employee, which together with any investment gains on
such savings provide the future pensions. Second, such
schemes are limited in their cover: only about one-half of the
current labour force of some 23 million are members. Third,
their terms and their benefits vary substantially from one
employment to another - the contribution rate, the level of
benefit, the 'guarantees' attached to that benefit and so on.
Fourth, they vary in the reliability of their finance - a matter
of some concern in financially difficult times. Finally, they
have varied (and continue to vary) in the extent to which they
are obliged to deliver their pension promises. These multiple
strengths and weaknesses are difficult to document - despite
some useful surveys from the Government Actuary's Department
- because they are private (Government Actuary, 1981). They
are increasingly interlinked with the prosperity or decline of
their company sponsors. So, in what follows it is more than

usually necessary to speculate on possibilities - the pursuit of what may happen - through a series of simplified models.

At this point we need to reiterate some of the factors raised earlier regarding the incidence of contributions, to determine who actually pays them. There is no fundamental difference between the individual contribution (from employer or employee) to the state or the company scheme: each is a 'tax' derived from wages or profits which (as part of the cost of the enterprise) is moved on to show up in prices. The only moderating factor is the income tax treatment of these contributions. Both the employee and employer contribution to the occupational scheme are tax deductible whereas in the state scheme, only the employer contribution can be offset against the employer's tax bill. This distribution is important, not least when it comes to the issue of 'contracting-out' of the state earnings-related scheme: the employee faces the option of a non-deductible contribution to the state or a contracted-out 'relieved' contribution to an occupational scheme.

Whatever such factors do to influence the choices which individuals and companies make with regard to contracting-out they may only obscure a much more substantial problem. What is the incidence of a tax relief? If government decides to make a pension contribution tax deductible, then it is choosing not to collect taxes on that sum: it incurs a tax expenditure, it forgoes a tax income. If this is income which government otherwise needs, then presumably that income deficit is made up elsewhere. Thus, to complete the equation, we need to know the source of the taxes which 'replace' those which have not been levied.

To further complicate things, replacements need not be taxes. The money could be borrowed, so that we would need to ask from whom it was borrowed and what funds (source) will be used to repay the loan? If this sequence seems 'circular' then we should not be surprised: resources move rather than stand still: prices and charges (including taxes) rarely stick where they are first imposed. What is surprising is that we have continued to believe and behave as if they did.

What then can we reasonably say about the origin of contributions to the occupational schemes? Well, first, to the vagaries of direct incidence (for instance, where do employers' contributions come from?) must be added those of indirect incidence. We have to make assumptions about the sources of the many indirect contributions made to pension schemes. These include tax reliefs, investment returns, 'bequests' from early leavers and finally, benefit guarantees.

First, there are the investment returns which the pension fund hopes to enjoy. If we assume, rather generously, that these returns are positive - where do these returns come from? Again, we can begin with a simple model. Assume an advanced funded scheme, with contributions flowing in from employers and employees and, for the moment, let us not concern ourselves with the origin of these direct contributions. With a forty-year advance funded approach it might be hoped that investment returns could provide between one-third and one-half of the final benefit costs. Let us assume that an efficient fund would generate enough investment income, compounded over the contribution years (and still earning during the benefit years) to exactly match the benefit promises in level and duration. That is, that contributions (A) plus earnings over contribution years (B) plus continued earnings over benefit years (C) - since all benefit is not instantly required - will match the total benefit outlay (D). In distributional terms the source of these earnings (B + C) can be crucial; they will constitute a substantial part of the final benefit and therefore their origin is central to any redistributive analysis. But, in all honesty, it is hard to say more than that they may be important. I know of no analysis within the economic or 'distributive' literature which identifies just where these borrowing costs fall: all that I shall do is to point to some possibilities.

If, in order to help procure a pension, I save part of my earnings and lend my savings to you, and you pay interest on these borrowings - then, you help pay for my future pension: you are a 'source'. You may be rich or poor. Less evidently, you may be a source as a taxpayer in a society which borrows heavily. Government borrowing may be repaid from current taxes: you may be one of the taxpayers. At a further remove, government may be borrowing from someone's pension fund - perhaps yours: then you may be the recipient of interest paid by government, via your taxes. Each time we buy goods from the shop which bought its premises (or stock) on borrowed money, then we play our humble part in debt repayment. The more that the 'pension fund' appears amongst the list of lenders, then the more of us are caught up in the process of repayment, and thus of redistribution, to current or future pensioners (which may include ourselves). The recurrent truth of the 1980s - and it should be no revelation - is that we are all debtors and creditors: we are all involved with banks, building societies, pension funds and governments, if often indirectly.

Whilst individuals pay interest directly, most borrowing, and thus the payment of interest is done by industry and by government. Industry must pay its borrowing costs out of trading profits which means that, like all other costs, they must work their way forward to consumers. If I purchase product X, I play some small part in repaying the capital loans of its manufacturer. In the final analysis, we need to identify the purchasers of the products in which the pension fund monies are invested.

If borrowers are various, so are the sources of investment returns and so, necessarily, are the 'financiers' of funded pensions. Imagine a pension fund with one-third invested in equities, one-third in properties and one-third in gilts: not an unusual situation. From whichever source - equities,

properties or gilts - we need to differentiate the redistributive
implications of an investment return by way of interest and one
by way of capital realisation. I may own £100 of shares and
receive £10 by way of shareholders' bonus: this £10 is derived,
as suggested, from company profitability (and its 'alternative'
distributions). But, I might put my £100 stock up for sale and
realise £110: the £10 profit would now derive from the stock
purchaser - whoever, he, she or it might be.

But, if we just consider the investment returns from share
bonus distributions, then the equity return is derived from
company trading profits, and must either be put down to
consumers or at one remove as diminished returns to shareholders or employees. It is impossible to generalise about who
bears this burden or in what degree: at best we might examine
the accounts of particular companies. In other words, with these
equity investments, we can note the potentially diverse sources
but will find it hard to pin them down. In so far as purchasers,
shareholders or wage earners have systematic characteristics
(rich/poor, young/old, etc.) then the investment returns would
at least reflect these distributions.

Then, there are the returns from property. These arise either
by way of income received as rents - on commercial, industrial
or residential properties - or, again, through the capital realisation, the sale, of the assets. Again, can we identify such
income sources when viewed as revenue? The rent met by the
individual tenant may be identifiable but the more elusive
problems are found when accounting for the rents paid by
private 'companies' or indeed by public authorities. The company presumably includes its rental costs in the price of its
goods or services to the consumer: the DHSS rents its private
office block and the costs are met by 'the government' - or,
more precisely, via its taxing or borrowing.

Finally, we have the return from gilts. We have alluded to this
phenomenon earlier. If government pays for borrowing, from
whom does it get the money? I have assumed that it comes
from taxpayers (income, indirect, VAT, etc.) but also from
borrowing (National Savings, SAYE, Premium Bonds and Treasury Stock). In each case we need to consider just who it is
who pays the taxes (and in what quantity) and who pays for
the borrowing (individuals, local authorities, others with minor
claims). From these elusive queries we turn now to consider the
dimension of time.

HOW LONG IN AND HOW LONG OUT?

The issue of the duration of wealth has already been raised:
it is obviously important in determining an individual's command
over resources. Whether the wealth you hold is judged flimsy
or robust by you, your bank manager, credit companies or the
like may well stem from its 'survival value'. In the case of
pensions and annuities, three major factors affect this valuation.

First is the likelihood that they will be paid: second, whether their value will be maintained and third for how long they will continue to be paid.

Longevity, compared with the years of contribution, and relative to other scheme members – is a major determinant of income transfers. In a system where benefits are payable for life, the longer-lived will receive more than their shorter-lived neighbours. This life expectancy may vary by occupational group, by sex and by marital status. If the insurer has anticipated this longevity then, in a risk-related scheme, those with higher expectations have paid more towards those greater benefits. Indeed, if the risk-rating were perfect, there would be no individual gain or loss and no transfer between individuals (except perhaps between the insured and the profit to the commercial insurance carrier). Resources would have been spread neatly, over time.

Access to such information on longevity, coupled with sufficient personal resources, might enable me to make provision for myself – but it would inevitably be wasteful. I would have had to provide for the extreme, for the possibility of long-term survival. In the final analysis it is the lack of personally predictable data which makes insurance so valuable a technique. But to return to the more common *pooled* insurance system (of state or occupational schemes) then pooling longevity will have substantial transfer effects. Changes in the respective life expectancy of men and women, of manual and non-manual workers, of the employed and the non-employed will each in turn modify the redistributive consequences of any benefit system. (Indeed, as was noted in the discussion of status transfers, between the single and the married, the relevant 'longevity' for any given contribution/benefit equation may be that of a spouse rather than the individual themselves.)

All will be compounded or potentially counter-balanced, if the contributory rules – especially on duration – are also modified. This is the neglected side of the redistributive equation, a further dimension of 'longevity' but which relates to the duration of contributions: for how long have you been contributing? We noted earlier that few income transfer systems are likely to be balanced in terms of years in and years out. In addition, British state pension schemes have been changing their membership requirements with every legislative change since pensions became contributory in 1926. Because of these changes no scheme has ever run its full term, but equally none has proscribed a contributory maximum (in years) other than by stating a starting age and age of permissible retirement. Within these limits the effective maximum has been some fifty years. Full benefit, however, could be achieved as a result of contributions from forty years. It follows that those who have exceeded this 'forty-year' requirement paid more than their 'fair share' into pensions. For instance, the male manual worker who retires today is likely to have joined the workforce when he left school at age fourteen: he will have featured as some kind of contri-

butor (by way of national insurance or taxpayer) from that
age onwards. In contrast to, say, the post-graduate medical
student he will have been paying for benefit for a long, long
time.

REDISTRIBUTIVE CONCLUSIONS AND CONSEQUENCES

Any serious student of this subject will be aware that it would
be possible to add, almost without end, to this list of factors
which affect the redistributive outcomes of any one pension
scheme. Not least, the tax treatment of contributions, of benefits and of the processes of funding and accrual, are of major
influence. I have explored these factors in some detail in other
writings so that they are deliberately neglected here (Reddin,
1977, 1981, 1982).

Likewise, the dynamisation of pension contributions and benefits, of maintaining their value in the face of inflation and
changing prices and incomes, involves substantial income transfers within both funded and pay as you go systems. The sources
of these transfers - who pays the interest which makes up the
investment return, who pays the current contribution used to
index a current benefit - are, as ever, hard to identify. The
issues of incidence which are involved with the funded schemes
have been identified in the earlier sections on the sources of
investment returns. In the case of PAYG schemes everything
depends on the source of the current contribution income - and
again, we have explored the problems of pinpointing such
'sources', which may go beyond their apparent incidence on
'employees' or 'employers'. One particular point which is worth
recording about the indexing of benefits is that, in general,
such indexing has been improving. In so far as these improvements have been enjoyed by current pensioners - who had not
'paid in advance' for such indexing - then there has been
another resource transfer in their favour.

The complex interactions of all these variables, not least when
most current contributors and many current beneficiaries have
membership of several pension schemes, will always be problematic to quantify. What we might note in conclusion is that the
level and structure of benefits in any one of these schemes is
likely to produce reactions in others.

Whilst the new state pension scheme suggests a positive
redistributive formula (its replacement ratios are inversely
related to income), its secondary characteristics have actively
encouraged the expansion of private pensions. Generous fiscal
reliefs (which now outstrip in scale and extent all other tax
allowances) and the generosity of the contracting-out conditions
have further stimulated occupational pensions which, given
their distribution, have further extended the inequality of old
age.

Likewise, in so far as state pension schemes have only offered minimal benefits this has doubtless contributed to some of the movement into occupational pensions in recent years. Thus, the choice of a pension formula in the state scheme has effects well beyond itself. Subsequently, there is likely to be a further reaction: as private provisions (apparently) prosper, the pressure to sustain or improve public provisions is emasculated. Not least, the pressure from the better-off will have declined. The higher taxpayer, now joined by humbler brethren, has been spurred on to choose tax-efficient routes to private salvation rather than seeing any joy in collective cures.

Such current divisions of welfare are, I would argue, likely to go on extending inequality in old age. Thus it is legitimate to criticise the current state pension scheme not just for its current and future 'direct' effects but for the related private distributions it will predictably generate. Thus, the very level of pension provision has redistributive potential. All of such effects are potentially changeable, but, to make the necessary changes requires more than political will. We have to begin with an awareness of these diverse interactions - something which has been sadly absent from most pension policy decisions.

PENSION WEALTH, ITS VALUE AND SIGNIFICANCE FOR THE ELDERLY: AN ADDENDUM

Any resource or benefit can have value without its being consumed. The fact that the benefit *will* be there if you need it is worth something. This is true of the unconditional benefit such as access to a health service in time of sickness: it is also true of conditional benefits, like insurance, where a previous contribution record is required but where benefit duration could be for a lifetime. Personal evaluation of these benefits will be related to our awareness of their existence and our anticipation of their receipt.

Benefits may be valued in terms of mental tranquillity, or because, once provided, they diminish our need or desire to purchase alternatives. Consider the valuation of a scheme of benefits guaranteeing income to my spouse and dependants should I die tomorrow. The value could be expressed in terms of the cash sum which they will receive between my death and their demise or independence (perhaps, less the contributions I had paid prior to my death). Alternatively, the value could be expressed in terms of the alternative costs and benefits if such cover had been made through another agency - for instance the cost of obtaining such cover privately in contrast to the public benefit. But something ought to be allowed for the sheer diminution of anxiety that such promises permit.

If at retirement you offer me the choice of a lump sum of £1,000 (which I might subsequently invest) or £100 per annum for life, then I can evaluate the alternatives in terms of estimated life expectancy and investment returns. But what the

annuity promises is to go on being paid until I die: if I exceed
my estimated life expectancy and live for another twenty years
I gain not just in future cash but today in avoiding risk. Whilst
I have not attempted to put a price on this 'risk removal' factor
- and presumably I might give it greater or lesser value at
different points in an individual's life - I do not mean to ignore
its existence.

There are many other levels at which the pension may be
valued. Some are current, some are future: all depend on who
makes them and on their perceptions and circumstances. An
individual may value the prospect of a future pension from an
employer whilst outsiders wryly observe that the prospect of its
realisation is remote. In other words, we may well have a dis-
parity of anticipatory valuations. Further, the process of
valuation is continuing - it may well vary as between pre-
retirement anticipation and post-retirement receipt (Scott,
1981).

Pensions can be valued at the family or household level. For
the dependent elderly, it might be the way in which they buy
their place in the domestic economy of the family, or confirm
their membership within it. In some households theirs could be
the only stable income around which others rise and fall.

From the perspective of the employee the pension may be
negatively valued: higher current wages might be preferred
to the higher contributions which the benefit demands. Alternatively, the employee may feel that s/he would be able to get
a better deal from a scheme other than the one in which they
are obliged to be a member.

Yet another valuation may be made by an employer: its potential to secure worker loyalty, its power to encourage people to
stay or to incorporate their commitment to the company. Further,
if the pension were funded it might be valued by a company or
the nation for its store of capital - to be used over the years
to create the industries of tomorrow. It will be part of that
golden cycle in which today's savings are the seed corn of
tomorrow, which in turn deliver the harvest, just when we need
it, in our own ripening years.

All these perceptions of pension value and their reliability
are related to the significance of income and wealth. This significance varies from one society to another, within a society
over time and it varies from one individual to another: we
cannot assume that wealth has a common relevance. For instance,
part of the 'significance test' for wealth concerns its duration.
Whereas most studies of wealth distribution record wealth-
holdings at a moment in time, the duration of that holding can
be crucial. Are we seeing one day of affluence in a life of
poverty or the opposite? Thus, we have to be alert to the movement of wealth and its susceptibility to change. As such, pension
wealth may be more or less stable than other wealth forms. In
part this stability (or potential for growth or decline) depends
on its financial foundations, but also - as noted - on the pro-

mises of others.

Wealth is usually portrayed as a store of resources, something currently held which can be consumed (like tins of food) or, reserved (like gold) which can be converted into usable resources. The conversion can be achieved directly by making the reserves liquid and buying things or indirectly by using them as collaterals for cash. Wealth can also exist in the form of promises. This can be a promise of future resources (in cash or kind), the promise to provide tomorrow's income or a future capacity to command goods or services when needed. Pension schemes provide a good example of these store (savings and funds) and promise (pay as you go) distinctions, although neither form is totally distinct. Investments are made against the promise of future returns: the PAYG contributor of today is effectively demanding that returns be made to him in the future. Yet all of such contracts and expectations are vulnerable: the store or the promise is never wholly secure. As such, all our pension futures will, in varying degree, be dependent on others (Barr, 1979).

Wealth is rarely of constant significance over an individual life-span. To be the holder of wealth may be more valuable in youth (to start a business, to buy a house) than to find prosperity whilst in the geriatric ward. If some income needs diminish with age (and if we assume some accumulation of assets over working life) then wealth in old age may be superfluous. Unless we rate highly the chance to bequeath wealth to others, there can be few reasons positively to encourage the retention of wealth in old age.

On the other hand, individuals may view their assets as their security. They will seek to maximise and maintain their reserves if they anticipate future costs, like a house needing repair or are anxious about the price of nursing care or funerals. They may also be 'hoarders' if they are not convinced of the security of their future income - whether from state pension, occupational benefit or savings. Conversely, a generous and credible pension scheme should help to diminish the need and the desire to maintain active saving throughout old age.

Whether the elderly experience any substantial change in their circumstances at retirement will depend on several factors. What will be the level of their retirement income (pension) relative to their previous (net) income? Will there be any increase or decrease in living expenses? Will there be changes in the tax-treatment of post-retirement income (compared with pre-retirement)? Will there be 'concessions' for the elderly: transport, entertainment, telephone, housing, health care, and so on?

All of these variables could be modified during the retirement years. A pension increase may be offset by a loss elsewhere, or a stable pension may be supplemented or eroded by changes in other benefits. A change in any one of these factors can alter the individual's real command over resources.

Finally, the resources of the elderly probably derive from more than one source. To focus exclusively on the range of state services and their inadequacy, whether pensions or housing for the aged, will miss the potentially complementary (or conflicting) role of other provisions. The private pension and the maintenance of its value, the presence of a strong voluntary sector, the role of supportive individuals (whether family or a wider community) will all contribute to the total state of wellbeing. Their absence may be more or less crucial to the prosperity of individuals. All will affect the significance of the income and the wealth they hold or expect: each in turn will be affected by the value of the pension benefit they receive.

Bibliography

Aaronovitch, S. (1981), 'The Road from Thatcherism', London, Lawrence & Wishart.

Agriculture Economic Development Council (EDC) (1977), 'Ownership of Land by Agricultural Landlords', NEDO.

Agricultural EDC (1978), 'Agriculture in the 1980s – the Impact of Taxation', NEDO.

Allen, R.C.D. (1965), 'Committee of Inquiry into the Impact of Rates on Households', Cmnd 2582, London, HMSO.

'Alternatives to Domestic Rates' (1981), Cmnd 8449, London, HMSO.

Atkinson, A.B. (1972), 'Unequal Shares: Wealth in Britain', London, Allen Lane.

Atkinson, A.B., ed. (1973), 'Wealth, Income and Inequality', Harmondsworth, Penguin.

Atkinson, A.B. (1975), 'The Economics of Inequality', Oxford University Press.

Atkinson, A.B., and Harrison, A.J. (1974), Wealth distribution and invest-ment income, 'Review of Income and Wealth', Series 20, no. 2.

Atkinson, A.B., and Harrison, A.J. (1978), 'Distribution of Personal Wealth in Britain', Cambridge University Press.

Barr, N. (1979), Myths my Grandpa taught me, 'Three Banks Review', December.

British Institute of Management (1977), 'National Management Salary Survey', Remuneration Economics Ltd.

British Institute of Management (1979), 'Business Cars', Management Survey Report No. 44.

British Institute of Management (1981), 'National Management Salary Survey', Remuneration Economics Ltd.

Brittain, J.A. (1960), Some neglected features of Britain's income levelling, 'Americal Economic Review', May.

Brittan, S. (1964), 'Treasury under the Tories', Harmondsworth, Penguin.

Britton, D.K., and Hill, B. (1975), 'Size and Efficiency in Farming', London, Saxon House.

Britton, D.K., and Hill, B. (1978), Differences in efficiency by size and tenure, Agricultural Economics Society Conference, December.

Bulmer, M. (1980), 'Social Research and Royal Commissions', London, Allen & Unwin.

Burghes, L. (1979), The old order, in Field (1979c).

Conservative Party (1976), 'The Right Approach to the Economy', London.

Cripps, F., et al. (1981), 'Manifesto', London, Pan Books.

Cronk, E. (1981), referred to in Behr, N., Commonwealth Valuation Confer-ence, in 'Commonwealth Association of Surveying and Land Economy', January

Crosland, A. (1967), 'The Future of Socialism', London, Cape.

Dean, A.J.H. (1978), Incomes policies and differentials, 'National Institute Economic Review', no. 85, August.

Department of Employment (1976), 'Gazette', July.

Department of Employment (1977), How individual people's earnings change, 'Gazette', January.

Department of Employment (1981), 'New Earnings Survey: 1981', part A, London. HMSO.

Department of Employment (1982), 'New Earnings Survey 1982', Part B, London, HMSO.

'Economic Trends' (1977), Developments in the statistics of the distribution of income, London, HMSO, December.

'Economic Trends' (1978), Personal Sector balance sheets, London, HMSO, January.

'Economic Trends' (1981), 'The distribution of income in the United Kingdom, 1978-9, London.

'Economic Progress Report' (1981), April, London, Treasury.

Edwards, C.J. (1978), The effects of changing farm size levels on fragmentation, 'Journal of Agricultural Economics', May.

Erritt, M.J., and Alexander, J.C.D. (1977), Ownership of company shares, 'Economic Trends', September.

Farm Management Survey (Annual), 'Farm Incomes in England and Wales', London, HMSO.

Field, F. (1979a), New disclosures on the rich, 'New Statesman', 17 August, p. 224.

Field, F. (1979b) 'One in Eight: a Report on Britain's Poor', London, Low Pay Unit.

Field, F., ed. (1979c), 'The Wealth Report', London, Routledge & Kegan Paul.

Field, F. (1981), 'Inequality in Britain: Freedom, Welfare and the State', London, Fontana.

Field, F., Meacher, M., and Pond, C. (1977), 'To Him Who Hath', Harmondsworth, Penguin.

Foster, C. (1981), 'Local Government Finance in a Unitary State', London, Allen & Unwin.

Foster, C.D., Jackman, R., and Perlman, M. (1980), 'Impact of Rates on Industry', London, Allen & Unwin.

'Future Shape of Local Government Finance' (1971), Cmnd 4741, London, HMSO.

Galbraith, J.K. (1977), 'The Age of Uncertainty', London, BBC/Andre Deutsch.

Government Actuary (1981), 'Sixth Report on Occupational Pension Schemes, 1979', London, HMSO.

Halsey, A.H., (1978), Class-ridden prosperity, 'Listener', 19 January.

Harbury, C. (1962), Inheritance and the distribution of personal wealth in Britain, 'Economic Journal', vol. 72, no. 288.

Harbury, C.D., and Hitchens, D. (1977), Wealth, women and inheritance, 'Economic Journal', March.

Harbury, C., and Hitchens, D. (1980), The myth of the self-made man, 'New Statesman', 15 February.

Harrison, A.J. (1979), Recent changes in the distribution of personal wealth in Britain, in Field (1979c).

Heddle, J. (1980), 'The Great Rate Debate', Conservative Political Centre, October.

Heller, R. (1974), 'The Common Millionaire', London, Weidenfeld & Nicolson.

Hill, B. (1980), 'Municipal Journal', 30 May.

Hill, S. (1978), The distribution of household income in the UK, 1963-1975, in Royal Commission on the Distribution of Income and Wealth, Volume of Evidence (1978).

Hird, C. (1979), The poverty of wealth statistics, in Irvine and Evans (1979).

House of Commons (1979), Minutes of evidence, Expenditure Committee, Session 1978-79, 26 March.

House of Commons (1981), 'Twelfth Report from the Committee of Public Accounts', 25 June.

Howe, Sir Geoffrey (1980), Budget statement, 'Hansard', 26 March.
Hugh-Jones, S. (1980), Should we abolish capital taxes, in 'Financial Weekly', 28 November.
Inland Revenue (1979), 'Statistics', London, HMSO.
Inland Revenue (1980), 'Statistics', London, HMSO.
Inland Revenue (1981), 'Statistics', London, HMSO.
Irvine, J., and Evans, J. (1979), 'Demystifying Social Statistics', London, Pluto Press.
Jackman, R., (1978) 'The Impact of Rates on Industry', CES, Policy Series 5.
Kay, J.A., and King, M.A. (1980), 'The British Tax System', 2nd edn, Oxford University Press.
Labour Party (1974) 'Manifesto', October, London.
Labour Research Department (1976), 'Labour Research', vol. 65, no. 8.
Layfield Report (1976), 'Local Government Finance', Cmnd 6453, London, HMSO.
'Local Government Finance' (1977), Cmnd 6813, London, HMSO.
Low Pay Unit (1981), Wealth tax changes in the 1981 budget, mimeograph.
Lund, P.J., and Hill, P.G. (1979), Farm size, efficiency and economics of scale.
MacAfee, K. (1980), A glimpse of the hidden economy in the national accounts, 'Economic Trends', London, HMSO, February.
Meade, J.E. (1978) (chairman of the Committee), 'The Structure and Reform of Direct Taxation', London, Allen & Unwin.
Muellbauer, J. (1978), Note on differential inflation in Royal Commission on the Distribution of Income and Wealth, Volume of Evidence (1978).
Nicholson, J.R. (1973), 'The distribution of personal income' in Atkinson (1973).
Northfield Report (1979), 'Report of the Committee of Inquiry into the Acquisition and Occupancy of Agricultural Land', Cmnd 7599, London, HMSO.
Piachaud, D. (1976), 'Prices and the distribution of incomes', London School of Economics, mimeograph.
Piachaud, D. (1978), 'Inflation and income distribution', in Hirsch, F., and Goldthorpe, J., eds, 'The Political Economy of Inflation', London, Martin Robertson.
Pond, C. (1977), Inflation, in Williams, F., ed., 'Why the Poor Pay More', London, Macmillan.
Pond, C. (1981), Low pay - 1980s style, 'Review No. 4', London, Low Pay Unit.
Pond, C., and MacLennan, E. (1981), 'Insuring poverty at work', London, Low Pay Unit.
Reddin, M. (1977), 'National insurance and private pensions: who gets what from whom?' in Jones, K., Brown, M., and Baldwin, S., eds. 'The Year Book of Social Policy in Britain, 1976', London, Routledge & Kegan Paul.
Reddin, M. (1981), Taxation and pensions, in Sandford, Pond and Walker (1981).
Reddin, M. (1982), 'Occupation, welfare and social division', in Jones, C., and Stevenson, J., eds, 'The Yearbook of Social Policy in Britain 1980-1', London, Routledge & Kegan Paul.
'Report on Non-Domestic Rates' (1980), Coopers & Lybrand Associates Ltd, February.
Revell, J. (1967), 'The Wealth of the Nation', Cambridge University Press.
Routh, G. (1980), 'Occupation and Pay in Great Britain, 1906-79, London, Macmillan.
Royal Commission (1955), 'On the taxation of profits and income', Cmd 9474, London, HMSO.
Royal Commission on the Distribution of Income and Wealth, Report No. 1 (1975), 'Initial Report on the Standing Reference', Cmnd 6171, London, HMSO.
Report No. 2 (1975), 'Income from Companies and its Distribution', Cmnd 6172, London, HMSO.
Report No. 3 (1976), 'Higher Incomes from Employment', Cmnd 6383, London, HMSO.

Report No. 4 (1976), 'Second Report on the Standing Reference', Cmnd 6626, London, HMSO.
Report No. 5 (1977), 'Third Report on the Standing Reference', Cmnd 6999, London, HMSO.
Report No. 6 (1978), 'Lower Incomes', Cmnd 7175, London, HMSO.
Report No. 7 (1979), 'Fourth Report on the Standing References', Cmnd 7595,
Report No. 8 (1979), 'Fifth Report on the Standing References', Cmnd 7679,
Volume of Evidence (1976a), Selected Evidence submitted to the Royal Commission for Report No. 1, London, HMSO.
Volume of Evidence (1976b), Selected evidence submitted to the Royal Commission for Report No. 2, London, HMSO.
Volume of Evidence (1976c), Selected evidence submitted to the Royal Commission for Report No. 3, London, HMSO.
Volume of Evidence (1978), Selected evidence submitted to the Royal Commission for Report No. 6, London, HMSO.
Background Paper No. 1 (1976), The financing of quoted companies in the United Kingdom: by Geoffrey Meeks and Geoffrey Whittington – a background paper to Report No. 2, London, HMSO.
Background Paper No. 1 (1976), Analysis of managerial remuneration in the United Kingdom and overseas; a report by HAY-MSL – a background paper to Report No. 3, London, HMSO.
Background Paper No. 3 (1977), The effects of certain social and demographic changes on income distribution: by Robert Dinwiddy and Derek Reed – a background paper to Report No. 5, London, HMSO.
Background Paper No. 4 (1977), The distribution of income in eight countries: by Thomas Stark – a background paper to Report No. 5, London, HMSO.
Background Paper No. 5(1978), The causes of poverty: by R. Layard, D. Piachaud and M. Stewart – in collaboration with N. Barr, A. Cornford and B. Hayes – a background paper to Report No. 6, London, HMSO.
Background Paper No. 6 (1978), Low incomes in Sweden: by John Greve – a background paper to Report No. 6, London, HMSO.
Background Paper No. 7 (1979), The distribution of wealth in ten countries: by Alan Harrison – a background paper to Report No. 7, London, HMSO.
Background Paper No. 8 (1979), A six-country comparison of the distribution of industrial earnings in the 1970s: by Christopher Saunders and David Marsden – a background paper to Report No. 8, London, HMSO.
Sandford, C. (1971), 'Taxing Personal Wealth', London, Allen & Unwin.
Sandford, C. (1979), The wealth tax debate, in Field (1979c).
Sandford, C. et al. (1973), 'An Accessions Tax', London, IFS/Heinemann.
Sandford, C., Lewis, A., and Pleming, C. (1978), Labour should think again about that wealth tax, 'Accountancy', September.
Sandford, C., Pond, C., and Walker, R., eds (1981), 'Taxation and Social Policy', London, Heinemann.
Scott, Sir B. (1981), 'Inquiry into the Value of Pensions', Cmnd 8147, London, HMSO.
Seers, D. (1951), 'The Levelling of Incomes Since 1938', Oxford, Blackwell.
Sutherland, A. (1980), Capital transfer tax and farming, 'Fiscal Studies', March.
Sutherland, A. (1981), CTT: An Obituary, 'Fiscal Studies', November.
Tawney, R.H. (1913), Poverty as an industrial problem, reproduced in 'Memoranda on the Problem of Poverty', London, William Morris Press.
Titmuss, R.M. (1962), 'Income distribution and social change', Allen & Unwin.
Titmuss, R.M. (1976), 'Commitment to Welfare', London, Allen & Unwin.
Townsend, P. (1979), Poverty in the UK, London, Allen Lane.
Treasury (1975), 'Wealth Tax', Cmnd 5704, London, HMSO.
Wainwright, R. (1981), 'An accessions tax', Liberal Party, London.
Ward, S. (1981), 'Pensions', London, Pluto Press.
Zuckerman, S. (1961), 'The Scale of Enterprise in Farming', Natural Resources (Technical) Committee, HMSO.

Index